Amanda French   Rachael Roberts   Joanne Ga█████ █████ Preshous

IELTS Foundation

Study Skills

a self-study course for all
General Training Modules

MACMILLAN

Macmillan Education
Between Towns Road, Oxford OX4 3PP
A division of Macmillan Publishers Limited
Companies and representatives throughout the world

ISBN 1-4050-8200-3

Text © Amanda French, Rachael Roberts, Joanne Gakonga
and Andrew Preshous 2005

Design and illustration © Macmillan Publishers Limited 2005

First published 2005

Original design and page make-up by Mike Cryer, eMC Design:
www.emcdesign.org.uk

Illustrated by Jim Eldridge (Beehive Illustration), Martin Sanders
(Beehive Illustration) and Tony Wilkins
Cover design by Andrew Oliver
Cover photograph by Photonica/Getty Images

Authors' acknowledgements
Amanda French would like to thank Liam Keane for his ongoing
support and encouragement.

Rachael Roberts, Joanne Gakonga and Andrew Preshous
would like to thank their families especially their spouses Chris,
Jack and Jo and their children Sam, Kinuthia, Mwathi, Laura
and Eleanor for all their support during this project.
Thank you to the many students at Solihull College who trialled
material and provided sample answers and valuable feedback.
And finally, thanks go to Sarah Curtis, Joe Wilson and the team
at Macmillan, whose faith in us and months of hard work helped
make the idea a reality.

The publishers would like to thank Paula Clossick, Lynn Clark,
Darren Conway and his IELTS class at Languages
International, Auckland (especially Sooyeon Bae and Wan-Lin
Chung), the staff and students of Harrogate Language
Academy (especially Charlie Martineau, Jessica Poole,
Marwan Salem Saeed Al Khatri and Amy Mun Yin Wu).

The authors and publishers would like to thank the following for
permission to reproduce their material:

Extract on paracetamol by Dr A D Emanuele taken from
PharmWeb (www.pharmweb.net), reprinted by permission of
the author.
Extract from 'Going Flatting' taken from
www.dbh.govt.nz/housing/tenancy/going-flatting, reprinted by
permission of the publisher.
Extract from 'Responsible Tourism Special' taken from
www.geographical.co.uk December 2003 copyright ©
Geographical 2003, reprinted by permission of the publisher.
Extract from 'New residents and visitors – driving in New
Zealand' taken from www.ltsa.govt.nz.
Extract from 'Student Services' taken from
www.pattisoncollege.com/student_serviceshtm.
Extract from 'Our stone age brain may simply be unable to cope
with the pace of modern life' by Roger Highfield first published
in *The Telegraph* 05.05.04 © The Telegraph 2004, reprinted by
permission of Telegraph Group Ltd.

Extract from 'Passing on the Salt' by Noel O'Hare first published
in *New Zealand Listener* 27.11.04, reprinted by permission of
more images.
Extract from 'Crowded House' by Olivia Kember first published
in *New Zealand Listener* 24.01.04, reprinted by permission of
more images.
Extract from 'Clever Canines' by Colin Woodward first published
in *The Chronicle* Vol.51 Issue 32. 15.04.05, copyright © Colin
Woodward 2005, reprinted by permission of the author.
Extract from *Lonely Planet Ireland 4* copyright © Lonely Planet
Publication 2004, reprinted by permission of the publisher.
Extract from 'The course' by Mark Story taken from *The New
Zealand Herald* 03.11.00.
Extract from www.englishforadults.co.uk , copyright © WF
Language Education & Travel, reprinted by permission of
Wendy Fitzgerald, WF Language Education & Travel.
Extract from 'The Race to Beat Stress' by Noel O'Hare first
published in *New Zealand Listener* 02.04.05, reprinted by
permission of more images.

The authors and publishers would like to thank the following for
permission to reproduce their photographs:
Alamy / Jeremy Pardoe p22, Alamy / Frances Roberts p24,
Alamy / Daniel Templeton p28; Corbis / Paul A. Sounders p27;
The Kennel Club p44; Photolibrary.com p12.

Printed and bound in Spain by Mateu Cromo

2009 2008 2007 2006 2005
10 9 8 7 6 5 4 3 2 1

Contents

Introduction

Welcome to IELTS Foundation Study Skills. This is a different kind of exam practice book. As well as providing you with exam practice materials, this book will:
- Familiarize you with the different question types you will find in IELTS and give you guided practice in each of them.
- Help you to develop the skills you need to be successful.

There are four parts, corresponding to the four IELTS modules. Each part begins with *skills development*. In these sections you will develop your skills through focused exercises, with detailed guidance given in the key to each question. Next, in the *skills practice* sections, you can put what you have learnt into practice. Finally, the book contains a complete *Practice test*.

As IELTS Foundation is aimed at students starting at around 4–5.5, some of the reading and listening texts are shorter or the questions are a little easier than you would find in IELTS, especially towards the beginning. Essential vocabulary is given in a glossary. This will support you as you gradually develop your skills and improve your IELTS score.

For Writing and Speaking both model answers and sample student answers are given, so that you can start to evaluate your own work. Useful language is also provided.

The book is intended to be used for self study, but could also form the basis of a short intensive IELTS preparation course.

The IELTS Exam

IELTS, or the International English Language Testing System, is an exam designed to assess your level of English, on a scale from 1–9. The score you need will depend upon the course and the university you want to study at, but many students find they need to get an overall band score of 6.

Each section is weighted equally, but it is possible to get half band scores for the Reading and Listening modules (eg 5.5, or 6.5), but only whole number bands (eg 5, 6, 7 etc) for Speaking and Writing. Overall, therefore, you may get a half band score.

Band 9 – Expert User
Has fully operational command of the language: appropriate, accurate and fluent with complete understanding.

Band 8 – Very Good User
Has fully operational command of the language with only occasional unsystematic inaccuracies and inappropriacies. Misunderstandings may occur in unfamiliar situations. Handles complex detailed argumentation well.

Band 7 – Good User
Has operational command of the language, though with occasional inaccuracies, inappropriacies and misunderstandings in some situations. Generally handles complex language well and understands detailed reasoning.

Band 6 – Competent User
Has generally effective command of the language despite some inaccuracies, inappropriacies and misunderstandings. Can use and understand fairly complex language, particularly in familiar situations.

Band 5 – Modest User
Has partial command of the language, coping with overall meaning in most situations, though is likely to make many mistakes. Should be able to handle basic communication in own field.

Band 4 – Limited User
Basic competence is limited to familiar situations. Has frequent problems in understanding and expression. Is not able to use complex language.

Band 3 – Extremely Limited User
Conveys and understands only general meaning in very familiar situations. Frequent breakdowns in communication can occur.

Band 2 – Intermittent User
No real communication is possible except for the most basic information using isolated words or short formulae in familiar situations and to meet immediate needs. Has great difficulty in understanding spoken and written English.

Band 1 – Non User
Essentially has no ability to use the language beyond possibly a few isolated words.

Band 0 – Did not attempt the test
No assessable information provided.

A summary of each module is outlined below:

Listening

The Listening takes about 40 minutes and each section gets progressively more difficult.

Part	Number of speakers	Number of questions	Situation	Example
1	2	10	social/general	Conversation between a student and a landlord
2	1	10	social/general	Welcoming talk for a group of new students
3	2–4	10	academic	students in a seminar discussion
4	1	10	academic	a university lecture

Question Types: multiple choice, completing notes or sentences, completing or labelling diagrams, charts or tables, classifying, matching and writing short answers.

Exam Tips: You will only hear each section ONCE. However, there is time to look briefly at the questions before each part is played. During the exam, you should write on the question paper, and at the end you will have 10 minutes to transfer answers to the answer sheet. It is important to do this carefully, and check grammar and spelling, as mistakes will lose marks.

General Reading

The Reading lasts one hour and there are three sections, of increasing difficulty, taken from newspapers, magazines, journals and any public information documents. Section 1 contains two or three texts – presenting the kind of 'everyday life' information that learners might see in an English-speaking country. Section 2 contains two texts which learners would read in an educational or training context. The text in Section 3 is longer and more complicated than those in Sections 1 and 2. Section 3 topics are of general interest, so learners do not have to be experts in the subject areas to understand them.

Question Types: multiple choice, choosing true/false/not given or yes/no/not given, identifying the views of the writer, completing sentences, completing a set of notes, a table, a summary or a flow-chart, classifying, matching, choosing paragraph headings, locating information and writing short answers. There are 40 questions in total.

Exam Tips: As with the listening module, answers are written on an answer sheet, but no extra time is given for this. It is important that you practise managing your time (20 minutes for each section) so that you can complete the whole module within the hour by reading quickly and efficiently.

General Writing

There are two tasks in this module and it lasts one hour.

Task	Time	Number of words	Description of task
1	20 minutes	At least 150 words	Write a short letter in response to the given situation or problem. The letter could be formal, semi-formal or informal.
2	40 minutes	At least 250 words	Write a discursive essay in response to a given argument, problem, situation or opinion. The style of the essay should be formal although the writer can also express their own views and refer to their experience.

Assessment: In order to do well in Task 1, you need to respond appropriately to all three given points. In order to do well in Task 2, you need to identify the topic and make sure the content of your essay is relevant. In both tasks, you are also assessed on how well you organize your answer; this includes the order in which your information is presented, your use of paragraphs and the way you show connection between ideas, sentences or clauses. You are also assessed on your range and appropriacy of vocabulary, and your range and accuracy of grammatical structures.

Exam Tips: It is important to keep to the timings, as Task 2 is longer, and carries more weight than Task 1. It is also important to keep to the word limits, as writing less than the number of words stated is likely to result in a lower score.

Speaking

The Speaking module takes between 11 and 14 minutes and is an oral interview between the learner and an examiner. It will be recorded on audio tape.

Part	Time	Description
1	4–5 minutes	General questions about home, family, studies, etc.
2	3–4 minutes	You are given a card with a topic and 3–4 prompt questions on it. You have 1 minute to prepare, and then have to speak for 1–2 minutes on that topic. At the end, the examiner may ask you a question.
3	4–5 minutes	Further discussion questions relating to the subject in Part 2. This section requires you to give opinions, speculate and express reasons.

Assessment: Assessment is based on your fluency, the range, and accuracy of the vocabulary and grammatical structures you use, and your pronunciation.

Exam Tips: Try to relax during the exam, and give more extended responses to questions rather than just 'yes' or 'no' to gain higher marks. You can prepare for this module, for example, by practising speaking for 1–2 minutes on different topics. However, don't memorize long speeches as examiners can usually spot this, and will ask you to talk about something else.

Study Skills: Listening

The Listening module is the first part of the IELTS exam. Do this quiz to see how much you know about it.

Quiz

1. How long is the Listening module in total?
   A about 30 minutes   **B** about 40 minutes
   C about 50 minutes
2. How many sections are there?
   A 4   **B** 5   **C** 6
3. How many questions are there in total?
   A 25   **B** 30   **C** 40
4. The first part of the Listening module is the easiest and the last part is the most difficult. True or false?
5. Each section is worth the same number of marks. True or false?
6. There are four situation types in the Listening module. Match the examples with a situation type (A–D). Then number the situation types (A–D) in the order you will hear them.

Adam telephones a restaurant to book a table for a party.
Professor Jones lectures on climate change.
Steve, Mary and Sarah discuss their assignment on water pollution.

Mr Green gives a talk on how to open a bank account in the UK.

- ❏ **A** a monologue (one person speaking) in a university situation, eg a lecture
- ❏ **B** a monologue relating to social needs, eg a speech about arrangements for meals at a conference
- ❏ **C** a dialogue (two people talking together) relating to social needs, eg a conversation about travel needs
- ❏ **D** up to four people talking together in an academic situation, eg a conversation between a tutor and a student about an assignment

7. How many times do you hear each section?
8. Do you have time to read the questions before you listen?
9. Where should you write your answers?
10. You will lose marks for incorrect spelling. True or false?

Section 1

Remember
- Read the **instructions** carefully so that you know what to do.
- Read the **questions** carefully and predict what you will hear.
- Think about **who** is talking, **where** they are and **what** the topic is. In the exam you will only have a short time for this, so do it as quickly as possible.

Skills development

Prediction

Listening module section 1: Exam information
Number of people: two (a dialogue)
Context: conversation about social needs
Example situation: a student applying for a parking permit or someone reporting a stolen bag

1 Read the questions. Think about:

- who is talking
- what they are talking about
- any other useful information

1. How long has Keiko been at the college?
   A a day
   B a few days
   C a couple of weeks

2. The main building
   A has three floors.
   B is by a lake.
   C has a glass front.

3. Which door should she take for the accommodation office?
   A the first on the left
   B the second on the right
   C the second on the left

2 📼 01 Listen and answer the questions.

Recognizing repetition and avoiding distractors

1 Read the recording script below. Which information is repeated?

Stephen: … when you get inside, go straight down the corridor, to the far end, and turn left. You'll see three doors on your left – accommodation is the middle one.
Keiko: So, I go along the corridor, turn left, and it's the second door on the left?
Stephen: That's right!

2 Look again at question 3. Why might someone choose B?

Completing notes

When completing notes, you will be given a word limit. You can write what you hear, but you might have to change the order of the words for the answer to make sense.

1 Rewrite these sentences. Write **NO MORE THAN THREE WORDS** for each answer. Check your answers are grammatically correct.

1 When you choose a university course, think about it carefully. It's a really important decision.

You need to .... before you choose a university course.

2 You might like to study near to your home town, or to go further afield.

It is usually possible to study .... or in another town or city.

3 The number of students who choose to study overseas is increasing very rapidly.

There has been a rapid rise in the number of students wanting to

....

2 Keiko made some notes about the accommodation available through the college. Read the notes and predict the kind of information you need to listen for.

3 📼 02 Listen and complete Keiko's notes. Write **NO MORE THAN THREE WORDS** for each answer.

4 Check your answers on page 81.

> *Three types of accommodation available:*
> ● *Home stay*
>   *Cost of home stay: (1) ....*
>   *per week with meals*
> ● *(2) ....*
> ● *Private lets*
>   *College makes sure flats are*
>   *(3) ....*

Remember
● Most information is not repeated, but if it is, you will usually hear it in different words (paraphrased), eg *studying overseas will **not be cheap**, in fact it could be **one of the most expensive** ways of getting qualifications.*
● In dialogues, information is sometimes repeated by another speaker to confirm something.

Remember
● Make sure you use the correct form of the words, and that your answers make grammatical sense.
● You will often have to change the words on the recording to fit the word limit grammatically, eg *It's not easy to find accommodation near the campus.*
*Accommodation near the campus is **difficult to find**.*

First name: Keiko

Surname: (4) ....

Nationality: (5) ....

Address: The Sunrise Guest House

(6) ....

Phone number: (7) ....

email address: keiko@hotmail.com

5 📼 03 Listen to the final part of the conversation between Keiko and the Accommodation Officer and complete the form.

> **Remember**
> **All** answers must be spelt and punctuated correctly.

> **Remember**
> Names of people and places always begin with capital letters. You will lose marks if you don't include them.

Listening for numbers and letters

1 📼 04 How do you say these numbers in English? Listen and check your answers.

15   50   162   £3.25   47%   0.54   12,651

2 📼 05 How do you say these letters in English? Listen and check your answers.

U   Y   J   O   G   X   I   P
Z   W   H   A   Q   R   E   B

3 📼 06 How do you say these punctuation marks in English? Listen and check your answers.

1 **/**

2 **-**

3 **:**

4 **;**

5 **.** (in web addresses)

4 📼 07 Listen and complete the notes with the appropriate words or numbers.

1 The man's name is ....

2 The answer is ....

3 The address is ....

4 Everest is ....high .

5 His name is ....

6 The address is ....

7 Her test score was ....

8 His favourite author is ....

9 The phone number is ....

10 The reference number is ....

11 The woman's name is ....

12 The address is ....

13 The web address is ....

14 The man wants to make an appointment with ....

15 The registration number is ....

Skills practice

Questions 1 and 2

📼 08 For questions **1** and **2**, listen and choose the correct answer.

1 How many people will be at Dan's party?
    A 10
    B 8
    C 18
    D 24

2 Which date does Dan book the party for?
    A 15th April
    B 16th March
    C 8th April
    D 16th April

Questions 3–5

While he was on the phone, Dan made some notes. For questions **3–6**, listen and complete the notes. Write **NO MORE THAN THREE WORDS** for each answer.

> For parties, the restaurant usually serves a (3) ....
> for a fixed price. There are three choices for each course, for
> example for starters there is prawn cocktail, soup or antipasto. At
> least one of the choices is (4) .... Also included
> in the price is (5) ....

Questions 6–9

For questions **6–9**, listen and complete the booking form.

GIOVANNI'S

Price per person: (6) £ ....

Deposit: (7) £ ....

Name: (8) ....

Phone number: (9) ....

Skills development

> **Listening module section 2: Exam information**
> Number of people: one (a monologue)
> Context: non-academic, social needs
> Example situation: an informal talk on how to open a bank account

Using key words for prediction

1 Read questions **1–3** below and <u>underline</u> the important words. Can you think of synonyms for these words?

2 ⌷ 09 Now answer questions **1–3**.

1 The programme
   A gives information about used car sales.
   B tells you the best way to buy a car.
   C tells you the most popular way to sell a car.
   D looks at different ways of buying a new car.

2 Which of the following reasons does the presenter give for someone wanting to buy a used car? Circle **THREE** letters **A–F**.
   A You are a new driver.
   B You have had an accident in your old car.
   C You don't have a lot of money.
   D Your old car is unreliable.
   E You want to learn to drive.
   F You need a bigger car.

3 One advantage of a dealer is
   A they have a lot of room to show you the cars.
   B they are cheap.
   C you have a legal right to return the car if something goes wrong.
   D they are honest.

Eliminating wrong answers

If you can eliminate even one or two wrong answers, you improve your chances of getting the right answer.

⌷ 09 Listen again and decide why the other answers to questions **1–3** above are wrong.

Completing a summary

1 Read this summary. For each gap, predict:

- the type of word missing (eg noun/verb/adjective)
- the kind of information it is asking for (use the context to help you)

A (1) .... way to buy a car is privately. Usually this is done by looking through the (2) .... and contacting the person selling the car directly. The (3) .... is that you will not get a warranty. If you are not knowledgeable about cars, you should have the car checked (4) .... You could also buy a car at auction. This could be very risky as you won't have (5) .... to inspect it properly before you buy it.

2 ⌷ 10 Listen and complete the summary.

Skills practice

Questions 1 and 2

11 Read through questions **1–3** and then listen and circle the appropriate letter.

1 What is Jenny Arnold's job?
   A Health and Safety Officer
   B Sports Coach
   C Health and Fitness Officer
   D Travel Agent

2 The subject of the lecture is
   A travelling.
   B staying safe and healthy abroad.
   C drawing classes.
   D summer holidays.

Question 3

Circle **TWO** appropriate letters.

3 Where does Jenny Arnold say you can get information about vaccinations?
   A from a hospital
   B from your doctor
   C from the Internet
   D from your local nurse
   E from NHS Direct

Questions 4–6

Read through questions **4–6** and complete the summary. Write **NO MORE THAN THREE WORDS** for each answer.

It is important to buy some (4) .... before you leave, even though it may be (5) .... , especially if you plan to do adventure sports. It will make your holiday more relaxing if you know that you could always (6) .... safely.

Questions 7–9

Read through questions **7–9** and then complete the sentences. Write **NO MORE THAN THREE WORDS** for each answer.

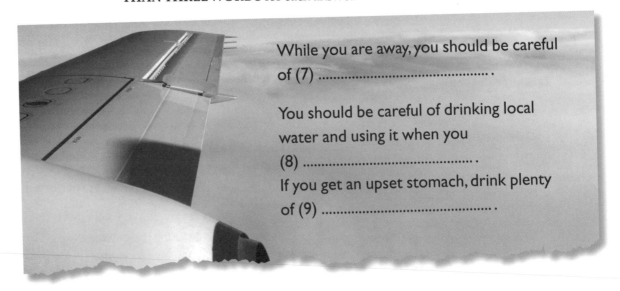

While you are away, you should be careful of (7) ....

You should be careful of drinking local water and using it when you (8) ....

If you get an upset stomach, drink plenty of (9) ....

Skills development

Listening for specific speakers

> **Listening module section 3: Exam information**
> Number of people: up to four people
> Context: education or training
> Example situations: a tutor and a student discussing an assignment, or a seminar situation with several students talking

[cassette] 12 Listen and answer the questions.

1 How many speakers are there in the conversation? How do you know?
2 What are their names?
3 How many times does each person speak?

Listening for specific information/short answers

Remember
- Listen for introductions at the beginning.
- Listen for any names that people use to direct the conversation.

1 Read the questions below and <u>underline</u> the key words. Which answer is a number? Which is a location or a situation? What *recent ecological problems* can you think of?

2 [cassette] 13 Listen and answer the questions. Write **NO MORE THAN THREE WORDS OR A NUMBER** for each answer.

1 Which **TWO** kinds of recent ecological problems does Anand mention?

   A ....

   B ....

2 What is the word limit for the assignment?

   ....

3 Where did Robert get his idea for a topic from?

   ....

Completing a table

Remember
- Use the time that you have before listening to the recording to look at the headings in the table. Then you can predict what you will be listening to.
- Look at the answers that are already in the table. These will help you to understand the type of answers required.
- Check if the numbering goes across or down the table.

1 Look at the table. Which questions ask you to identify types of pollution? Which answer is a date?

2 [cassette] 14 Listen and complete the table. Write **NO MORE THAN THREE WORDS** for each answer.

Pollution problem	Solution provided by	Completed
(1)	City Council	(2) ....
Boat traffic	(3)	next year
(4)	(5)	ongoing project

Classifying

For classification tasks, you have to match statements to one of three options. There may be more than one statement for each option.

1 Write the words in the box in the appropriate place in the table.

waste water
jet ski/motor boat fuel
rain and wind   crab
blown   marine life

Sea creatures	Stormy weather	Sewage	Emissions

2 Look at the question below and <u>underline</u> the key words.

3 🎞 15 For questions **1–4**:

if they refer to   Sewage   write   **S**
                      Boat traffic   write   **B**
                      Rubbish   write   **R**

Remember
You may have to use several options more than once.

1   Which kind of pollution can be used by sea creatures? ....
2   Which kind of pollution gets worse in stormy weather? ....
3   Which kind of pollution is increasing? ....
4   Which kind of pollution makes Sydney's population most upset? ....

Spelling

As in Section 2, sometimes words are spelt out for you, but often they are not. Even if the words are not spelt out, you must still spell them correctly.

1 🎞 16 Listen and complete the sentences.

1   The college is on the .... of an old castle.
2   The meeting will be held on ....
3   Please hand your essays in by next ....
4   We .... that you take the test in May.
5   The course is .... and highly beneficial.
6   .... rose dramatically in 2001.
7   I would .... you to do your homework.
8   He was a very successful ....
9   Different .... have different management systems.
10 He had a very .... career.
11 Studying abroad can help you become more ....
12 .... unwanted emails, or *spam*, is a growing problem.

2 Now check your answers on page 83.

2 Now check your answers on page 83.

3 Here is a list of words common in academic writing. Which **THREE** are spelt wrongly? Use your dictionary to check form and meaning.

accompany   constent
evident   percieved
suficient   specified

Skills practice

Questions 1–4

🔊 17 Complete the table. Write **NO MORE THAN THREE WORDS OR A NUMBER** for each answer.

	'A' Levels	Foundation Course
Length of course	2 years	1 year
Number of subjects studied	2–3	(1) ....
English language support given	often none	(2) .... per ....
Main type of assessment	exam(s)	(3) ....
Most popular with	(4)	overseas students

Questions 5–8

Write **NO MORE THAN THREE WORDS OR A NUMBER** for each answer.

5   What kind of English does Cathy study? ....

6   What does she say is different to her language? ....

7   Cathy studies the following modules:
   • economic theory
   • marketing strategies
   • ....

8   What does Brenda think about Cathy's course? ....

Questions 9–12

For questions **9–12**:
if they refer to   Millford University   write **M**
                      Ainsley University   write **A**
                      Parmouth University   write **P**

9   Which university has given Cathy a conditional offer? ....

10   Which university usually requires an IELTS score of 6.5? ....

11   Which university has a good reputation for Business Studies? ....

12   Which university is in a good location? ....

Skills development

Labelling a diagram with numbered parts

> **Listening module section 4: Exam information**
> Number of people: one (a monologue)
> Context: education or training
> Example situation: a lecture. The subject may be quite specific, but remember that you do not need any specialist knowledge to answer the questions.

1 Look at the following three diagrams.

1 Which one shows a plan or map?
2 Which one shows a process?
3 Which one shows an object?

Diagram 1

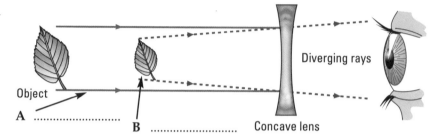

Diverging rays

Object

A ....

B ....

Concave lens

Diagram 2

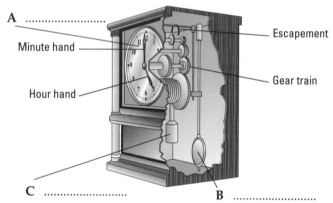

A ....

Minute hand

Hour hand

Escapement

Gear train

C ....

B ....

Diagram 3

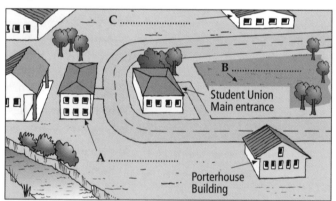

C ....

B ....

Student Union
Main entrance

A ....

Porterhouse
Building

2 🔲 18 Now listen and complete the labels on the diagrams.

3 Look at diagram 4. What does it show? Describe the positions of the numbered parts.

Remember
Study the diagram. Note what it shows and what positions things are in.

4 🔲 19
Listen and complete the labels. Write **NO MORE THAN THREE WORDS** for each answer.

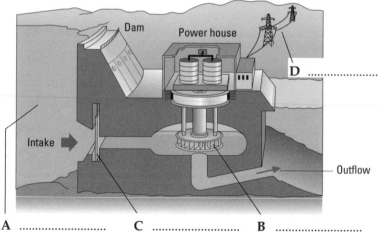

Dam

Power house

D ....

Intake

Outflow

A ....   C ....   B ....

Labelling a flow chart

1 Look at the flow chart below. Which answer is a number?

2 📼 20 Complete the flow chart. Write **NO MORE THAN THREE WORDS OR A NUMBER** for each answer.

GENERATOR	❏ **Create power**
TRANSMISSION SUBSTATION Power at **1** .... volts	❏ **Transforms electricity to high voltages**
LOCAL POWER SUBSTATION Power at 7,200 volts	❏ **Reduces voltage** ❏ **2** .... ❏ **Can turn off power if necessary**
TRANSFORMER BOX/DRUM Power at 240 volts	❏ **Lowers power to make it suitable for 3** .... **service**
CIRCUIT BREAKER/FUSE BOX	❏ **Safety device to minimize 4** ....

Sentence completion

1 Is the information you need in the sentences below a noun, a verb or an adjective?

1 Two positive aspects of hydroelectricity are that it is .... and ....

2 One limiting factor of hydroelectricity is that it requires ....

2 📼 21 Listen and answer the questions.

Listening for signpost words

Signpost words are words or phrases that tell a listener what the speaker is going to talk about next, eg *Right*, or *Anyway* indicate a change of subject and *for instance* indicates when the speaker is going to give an example.

Look at these extracts from the lecture on hydroelectricity. What do the <u>underlined</u> words indicate?

1 <u>I want to move on</u> today <u>to</u> a form of power that many would argue is far superior.
   A contrasting information
   B introducing a new topic
   C summing up

2 Right, <u>as you can see</u>, under the dam there is a control gate …
   A introducing a new topic
   B drawing attention to a visual
   C emphasising a point

3 <u>As we've said</u>, the power leaves the generator and enters …
   A recapping or reviewing information
   B summing up
   C adding extra information

Skills practice

Questions 1–4

🔲 22 Complete the sentences below. Write **NO MORE THAN THREE WORDS OR A NUMBER** for each answer.

1 Oil formation began between 10 million and .... years ago.

2 Dead plankton sank to the sea bed to mix with the ....

3 Layers of sediment put pressure and .... on the source rock.

4 Oil collects in porous rock, eg ....

Questions 5–7

Complete the diagram below. Write **NO MORE THAN THREE WORDS** for each answer.

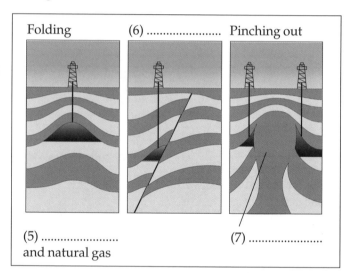

Folding   (6) ....   Pinching out

(5) .... and natural gas   (7) ....

Questions 8–12

Complete the flow chart using **NO MORE THAN THREE WORDS** for each answer.

Initial stages	Preparation for drilling	Drilling
Legal issues are settled.	Land is cleared and levelled. (8) .... may be built. A well is dug or a source of local (9) .... is found. Large, plastic-lined hole called a (10) .... is made. A *cellar* is dug at the site of (11)	Main hole begun with smaller drill. (12) Main rig is ....

Study Skills: Reading

How much do you know about the IELTS General Training Reading module? Do the quiz below to find out.

Skills development

The IELTS Reading module tests different reading skills. You already have these skills when you read texts in your own language and you should train yourself to use them when reading texts in English. The type of skill we use depends on the type of text; for example, we use our ability to scan a timetable or a newspaper article to find information that we need. We may skim read a magazine feature or an article in a business journal to see what the general topic is about. The table below gives examples of which reading skill you might find helpful for different IELTS tasks.

EXAMPLE OF IELTS TASK	SUGGESTED READING SKILL
Matching tasks: for example: p.24 Section 1 Text 3 p.26/27 Section 1 Text 4	Scanning = reading a text quickly/not every word or line/to find the information or details you need
Headings for each paragraph/section: for example: p.22/23 Section 1 Text 2	Skimming = reading a text quickly/not every word or every line/to see what the general topic or themes are
True/False/Not given: for example: p.29/30 Section 2 Text 1	Intensive reading = reading a text slowly and carefully/to understand the ideas and meaning in each sentence

You should try these different skills and find out which of them works best for you for each text and task type. But an important thing to remember is the time pressure when you take an IELTS test. You should spend about **20 minutes** on each **section**, and you won't have time to read everything in an intensive way!

When you do the reading tests, check the time you spend on each one.

**Section 1,
Reading Text 1**

Remember
- A short-answer task follows the order of the information in the text. This should help you locate the right answer.
- Read the instructions carefully : sometimes you can write only two words and sometimes three words. Sometimes you can write a number.
- This type of task tests factual information.

Short-answer questions

Look at Section 1, Reading Text 1 below about paracetamol, a medicine often used to treat adults and children.

Answer the questions below using **NO MORE THAN THREE WORDS AND/OR A NUMBER** for each answer.

1 What does paracetamol reduce?

2 What is the best way for young children to take paracetamol?

3 After what treatment should young children take paracetamol?

4 Who should get a doctor's advice about taking paracetamol?

5 What is the maximum amount of paracetamol tablets an adult can safely take in 24 hours?

6 How often can a child safely take paracetamol?

Section 1, Reading Text 1

Paracetamol

is the most widely accepted medicine for the relief of pain and fever; these symptoms can diminish* within ten minutes of taking paracetamol. It can either be a medicine prescribed by a doctor or it can be purchased as an over-the-counter medicine in retail pharmacies.

Paracetamol and its combinations are mainly available as tablets for immediate consumption or for dissolving in water before consumption. They are suitable for most people including the elderly and young children and can be taken by people who are sensitive to aspirin or who are suffering from asthma.

Paracetamol in liquid form is particularly suitable for young children, and can be given to babies to treat the raised temperature that may follow immunization against usual childhood diseases. Paracetamol products can normally be used by pregnant women although it is wise to ask your doctor about taking any medicines at this time.

The recommended dosage of paracetamol in adults is two 500mg tablets every four to six hours, not exceeding eight tablets in any 24 hour period. This dosage may be continued for several days.

Children's dosages vary with the age of the child and the type of product, therefore the instructions on the pack should always be followed. In general, children's dosages are based on a single dose of 10mg paracetamol per kilogram bodyweight, which can be repeated 6 hourly, not exceeding four doses per 24 hours.

Glossary
diminish = to become less

Skills practice

Paraphrasing

Paraphrasing means that you say or write something in a different way, so it has the same meaning. For example:

(a) original sentence: *I intend to sit the IELTS test in four weeks' time.*
    paraphrase: *Next month, I'm going to take IELTS.*

(b) task question: What is the best way for young children to take paracetamol?
    text: Paracetamol in liquid form is particularly suitable for young children.

The ability to recognize a paraphrased sentence or a group of sentences will help you with all the tasks and texts in the IELTS test.

1 Look at the statements below. Decide if (a) or (b) is a more suitable paraphrase.

1 Travel costs will be reimbursed only when receipts can be provided.

   (a) We will pay for your journey if you can prove what you paid for it.

   (b) It is important that you choose the cheapest means of transport to get there.

2 You will receive a 5% discount if the electricity bill is paid 10 days in advance of the deadline.

   (a) Pay your bill 10 days before the final day if you want to pay less for your electricity.

   (b) If payment for your electricity bill is more than 10 days late, you will have to pay 5% extra.

3 Photography is prohibited in the special exhibitions at the museum.

   (a) You need permission if you want to use your camera in an exhibition room.

   (b) You are not allowed to take photographs of any of the special exhibits.

4 Maps and sandwiches for the trek can be provided on request.

   (a) We will give you maps and sandwiches for the trek if you ask us.

   (b) It is a good idea to bring your own maps and sandwiches for the trek.

5 This medicine may cause mild side effects such as headaches and dizziness.

   (a) Take this medicine to prevent headaches and dizziness.

   (b) You could suffer from headaches and dizziness if you use this medicine.

6 The library will remain open during the public holiday on Monday 1st May.

   (a) The library will close on the public holiday and open again on Monday.

   (b) The library will not close on Monday 1st May.

Flat-hunting

A

You have decided to move into a flat. The first thing you need to do is your sums – before you commit to anything. As an example, if your rent is $120 per week, then you may need 4 weeks' rent as bond and 2 weeks' rent in advance. That's $720 in total before you even move in.

B

Often friends or colleagues know of a vacant place but otherwise there are other things to try. Read through the "To Let" column in your local newspaper. You could put an advertisement in the window of your local corner shop saying that you are flat-hunting and leaving your contact details. Some real estate agents also have rental flats available.

C

Once you've found a flat, you should get a tenancy agreement, which is a contract between you, the tenant*, and the landlord. It sets out what you and your landlord each agree to do. Every tenancy agreement must be signed by both you and the landlord, with a copy held by each of you.

D

You and the landlord will work out when, where and how you'll pay the rent. The landlord must give you a receipt for the rent you pay. If you are using automatic payments or a not-negotiable personal cheque, the bank records act as receipts. You will usually be asked to pay rent in advance.

E

If you are a flatmate rather than a tenant, you may have different rights. Tenants are responsible to the landlord for the whole of the rent and any damage done. If you have an agreement with a landlord, you're a tenant. If someone signs the agreement and then allows you to share the flat you are a flatmate. Only landlords can ask tenants to leave, but a flatmate can be asked by the tenant.

F

Should you have any problems regarding your tenancy, you can contact *Tenancy Services*. They will provide you with advice about your rights and obligations and you can then decide on the next step to take. If you cannot resolve the matter with the landlord, their trained mediators will try and help you both settle the dispute.

G

It is up to you to pay the rent on time and keep the premises reasonably clean and tidy. You must notify the landlord as soon as any repairs are needed. You should not exceed the number of occupants stated in the tenancy agreement.

Glossary

a tenant = a person who pays rent for a flat or house directly to the landlord

Matching headings to paragraphs

The public information document 'Flat-hunting' on page 22 has seven sections (**A–G**).

Choose the correct heading for each section from the list of headings below.

List of headings
- i   The tenant's responsibilities
- ii   Changes to payments
- iii   Sorting out financial agreements
- iv   What to do after you've asked around
- v   Your legal position once you're in the flat
- vi   Asking the right questions
- vii   Make sure the arrangement is in writing
- viii   Sorting out disagreements
- ix   Work out what you can afford
- x   The facilities you should expect

Skills practice

Skimming to find the general theme

Quickly read the three texts A, B and C below. Match the texts to a heading i, ii, or iii. The vocabulary in each text should help you decide.

i   The facilities you should expect
ii   Changes to payments
iii   Make sure the flat will suit your needs

Vocabulary development

Now use the words to complete the paragraphs below. You may need to change the form of some of the words.

know (v)   provide (v)
higher (adj)
fully-furnished (adj)
alter (v)
fortnightly (adv)
find out (phrasal verb)
set up (phrasal verb)
enquire (v)
neighbours (n)
permit (v)   right (n)
amount (n)

A   A landlord has no (1) .... to increase your rent once a certain (2) .... has been agreed. In New Zealand, rent for residential property is usually paid (3) .... but check that this is in your contract. If so, the landlord cannot demand weekly rent at a later date and nor can a tenant (4) .... the schedule of direct debits they have (5) .... with their bank.

B   It is worth (6) .... who your immediate (7) .... would be: consider their likely active hours and noise. You could also (8) .... whether the property has ever been broken into and you should (9) .... whether the landlord objects to pets, and whether friends or family would be (10) .... to stay.

C   In New Zealand, all flats and houses must come with a cooker but this is the limit to the whiteware landlords are obliged to (11) .... Bathrooms may or may not have a bath but must at least have a shower. It is possible to rent (12) .... flats or houses but the rent will be considerably (13) ....

Summerfield Community Centre
Events in May

A <u>Bang the Drum!</u>
The first time this music class is being offered to children in Summerfield.
No booking necessary – just turn up! If popular, it will become a regular class. £2 per child.
Monday 2nd 10 a.m. – 11 a.m. Room 2

B <u>Yoga</u>
This class continues to run at these times:
Beginners   Tuesdays   7–8 p.m.
Intermediate   Wednesdays   7.30–8.30 p.m.
Advanced   Saturdays   10–11 a.m.
£6 for an hour's class. All ages welcome.
(Crèche available for children)
Bring towel and bottle of water.   Room 3

C <u>Cookery class</u>
Ying Zhang Xue is head chef at the Canton Café. For just £5, he will show you how to prepare some delicious and nutritious dishes.
Thursday 12th 7.30 p.m. Room 3
Tickets must be purchased in advance at reception.

D <u>Book Fair:</u>
Once again we are hosting the book fair. If you have any books to donate, please leave them at reception no later than 12th May.
There will be a small entrance charge.
Saturday 14th 9.30 (in the Hall)

E *<u>On the beach</u>*
Written by Craig Bailey, this play deals with childhood experience and adult memories. Violent scenes mean it is unsuitable for children. Opening night is Friday 21st (8 p.m.) before a national tour begins.
Tickets on sale now (£20). The Hall

F <u>Concert</u>
Enjoy an unforgettable evening of traditional blues music from *Days Gone By*. The band has performed to audiences all over the country. If the good weather lasts, the concert will be in the Community Centre garden. Otherwise it will take place in the hall: Sunday 23rd 6 p.m.
Tickets £10

G <u>Summerfield – a history</u>
Local historian Jenny Grove will give a free talk and slide show on the history of our town. Copies of Grove's book *Reflections* (£25) will be on sale afterwards.
Wednesday 26th 8 p.m. Room 3.

Section 1, Reading Text 3

Multiple matching: Matching options to extract

Look at the seven events (**A–G**) above.

For which event are the following statements true?

1   It is necessary to buy tickets before the day of the event.
2   It is not recommended that children attend this event.
3   It is suitable for different levels of ability.
4   It costs nothing to attend this event.
5   It will happen again if enough people like it.
6   It may have to take place in another location.

Remember
- This type of matching task does not follow the order of information in the text.
- Do not choose a letter for an answer more than once unless the instructions say it is possible.

Skills practice

Guessing the meaning of words

The English language has over 600,000 words, not including specialized scientific terms! When native English speakers read articles in newspapers and magazines, they may see a word they've never seen before. This is usually not a problem because they can often guess the meaning of the word by:

- looking at the surrounding context (the meaning of the rest of the sentence or paragraph can help you work out the probable meaning of a single word or phrase)
- recognizing the part of speech (if you know that a word is a noun, adjective, verb, adverb, etc. you can see how it fits/affects the surrounding words)
- noticing prefixes (every prefix has a general meaning eg sub=under, re=again)

You probably do this, too, in your own language. Try to do it in English.

Recognizing part of speech

1 Look at the adjective column below. All the words are from the text and questions on Summerfield Community Centre. You can see some of them share the same endings. Complete the rest of the table.

Noun	Verb	Adjective	Adverb
		popular	
		regular	
	no verb	delicious	*old-fashioned and rare use*
	no verb	nutritious	
		national	
	no verb	traditional	
	verb has a different meaning	violent	
		different	
		(un)suitable	
		(un)forgettable	
		free	
		necessary	

Guessing the meaning from context

2 Below are three extracts from an article on how to be a responsible tourist. Read the following extracts to see if you can understand their general meaning. Then guess what the underlined words mean. You can do this by:

- using your general knowledge and common sense about a subject
- looking at the rest of the sentence or paragraph
- recognizing the part of speech
- replacing the underlined words with a word/phrase you think has the same meaning

Responsible Tourism

Read up before you go. Find out a little about your (a) <u>destination</u> before traveling. Not only will this (b) <u>enable</u> you to make more (c) <u>informed</u> decisions about where to go and what to see, but having an idea of the political and social context of a place will reduce the possibility of your unknowingly (d) <u>colluding</u> in environmental
5   destruction and causing problems for local people.

a   What does *destination* mean? Look at the title, the sub-heading of extract 1 and the context in line 0.
b   How can you divide *enable* into a prefix and a verb? Replace the prefix with a verb.
c   What part of speech is *informed*? What is the noun of this word? What does an *informed decision* mean?
d   What does the prefix *co-* usually mean? Read the rest of the sentence after *colluding*. Do you think *colluding* has a positive or negative meaning? Replace *colluding* with a short phrase with a similar meaning.

Photography. Eighty per cent of people in a UK survey said they would (e) <u>object</u> if rich tourists came and took their photo without permission. Ask first, and if the person you want to photograph looks away or says 'no', then (f) <u>refrain</u>. Be careful not to use flash photography inside museums or places where it could damage
10   (g) <u>fragile</u> surfaces.

e   Read the first sentence in line 6 + 7. How would you feel if a tourist took photos of you without permission? What part of speech is *object* and what does it mean?
f   What should you do if someone says 'no' when you want to take their photo? Replace *refrain* with a short phrase with a similar meaning.
g   What part of speech is *fragile*? What kind of surface could be damaged if people take photographs of it?

Trekking and Camping. Keep to paths when trekking, especially in fragile mountain areas. Walking outside the path causes (h) <u>erosion.</u> Camp in (i) <u>designated</u> areas where possible, and in other places seek permission from
14   the local landowner and (j) <u>ensure</u> that you aren't disturbing wild or farm animals.

h   What part of speech is *erosion*? What happens to the ground if people keep walking on it? Replace *erosion* with a short phrase with a similar meaning.
i   What part of speech is *designated*? What is the verb of this word? What does a *designated area* mean?
j   How can you divide *ensure* into a prefix and a verb? Replace the prefix with a verb.

Section 1, Reading Text 4

Remember
- This type of matching task does not follow the order of the information in the text.
- Read questions 1–6 and underline the key words. Then skim or scan the text for ideas or words you think could be connected to the question.

Matching options to paragraphs/sections

The passage has eight sections labeled **A–H**.

Which section mentions the following?

1   the reason why some people do not need to take the whole driving test
2   an example of how driving rules are different in New Zealand
3   the conditions that need to be fulfilled before someone can work as a driver
4   behaviour that could lead to a person's licence being taken away
5   the procedure required if someone is believed to have a certain disability
6   a restriction on what kind of vehicle a person is allowed to drive

New residents and visitors – driving in New Zealand

A

If you have an overseas driver licence or international driving permit you can drive for one year after you first arrive in New Zealand. If you do not have one of these you must apply for a New Zealand driver licence. You can only drive the types of vehicles covered by your overseas driver licence or international driving permit.

B

If you want to earn a living from driving you will probably need to convert to a New Zealand driver licence first and then get a driver licence endorsement. For example, you have to complete courses, pass exams and have a police check before you can earn money carrying passengers or drive a truck.

C

All drivers must know the road regulations and signs. Learning these is particularly important because of our unique 'Give Way' regulation (you must give way to vehicles coming from the opposite direction and turning right, when you are turning left). You can find out more about this when you study the Road Code.

D

Some countries require similar driving skills and have similar licensing systems to New Zealand's so drivers from these countries may not have to sit the practical driving test. If your licence comes from Australia, Canada, Norway, a member state of the European Union, South Africa, Switzerland or the United States of America, you don't have to sit the practical test.

E

If you fail the test, you can still use your overseas licence or permit if you have been here for less than one year. You can apply to sit the test again. If you fail the practical test after a year you must be accompanied by someone who has held a full driver licence for at least two years until you pass.

F

In New Zealand you must carry your licence or permit at all times when you are driving. If your overseas licence or permit is not in English we suggest you carry an official translation with you (a translation from an official source, eg a translation service or language centre).

G

Your eyesight will be checked when you apply for a new licence. An eyesight machine will check how well you can see at a distance and to the sides. If the check detects a problem you will need to present an eyesight or medical certificate before your licence can be issued.

H

Roadside Licence Suspension means the police seize a driver's licence and immediately suspend them from driving for 28 days. This can happen if you are caught driving at more than double the legal alcohol limit or are caught speeding at more than 50km/h above the limit

Skills practice

Multiple-matching tasks

You might see a multiple-matching task in any section of the Reading module, but in Section 3, the task will be more difficult. You may need to look for 'an example of' or 'a description of' or 'a reason for', etc. in the different paragraphs.

Look at the words/phrases on the left and match them with an extract on the right.

1 a **means/a way** of obtaining animals for zoos	a Nowadays we have access to exotic animals through television documentaries but in the past, the only way people could experience them was by a visit to the zoo – an exciting day out for the whole family.
2 **conditions** that zoos must fulfil to take care of their animals	b If many zoos do close down, it will mean that far fewer people will have the chance to have close contact with exotic animals.
3 an **explanation** for the popularity of zoos	c Zoos must ensure the living areas of their animals are large enough for them to explore and clean enough for them to remain healthy.
4 a **disadvantage**/a **drawback** of not having zoos	d Many animals are captured by hunters in their natural habitat and shipped across the world to a different continent.
5 an **improvement** that zoos have made	e Zoo-born chimpanzees cannot simply be let free to go back into the wild. First they are taken to a huge enclosure at the edge of the forest. Here they need to learn how to find food for themselves and build their own nests. Human contact is reduced every day.
6 a **justification** for the existence of zoos	f Over the last few decades, many cages have been replaced by larger enclosures which provide the animals with a more natural environment.
7 **evidence** of the bad effect zoos have on animal behaviour	g It is often said that without zoos many animals themselves would no longer survive. In the wild, they would have been hunted to extinction.
8 a **procedure** for releasing animals into their natural environment	h You can still see animals pacing backwards and forwards along the same path for hours. Some animals pull out their own fur while other animals refuse to eat.

True/False/Not given

Do the following statements agree with the information given in Section 2, Reading Text 1?

Write:

TRUE	if the statement agrees with the information given
FALSE	if the statement contradicts the information given
NOT GIVEN	if there is no information about this

1 If students want to use a computer, it is necessary to book a time slot.
2 It is possible for students to find out the name of their personal counsellor before Orientation Day.
3 Students from other colleges can put up advertisements for flatmates at Pattison College.
4 Students can ask Pattison College to book accommodation for them at a hotel.
5 Pattison College can arrange for students to be insured immediately through the BC Medical Services Plan.
6 Students can be collected from the airport and be taken to any kind of accommodation they have organized.
7 Canada Swan Travel can help students prepare the documents they need to get a visa.

Section 2, Reading Text 1

Student services

Internet access
Pattison College has two computer rooms that are used for classes at all levels. There are also several computers with internet access located in student areas, for student use only. This means that students can maintain e-mail contact with their family and friends from the College's computers, practice English and research information in the computer rooms.

Counselling
Students who need help to plan their studies, to deal with homestay issues, or with personal problems will find there are several staff available to assist them. There are staff members who deal primarily with student issues, who focus on the courses, and who work with students in the ESL programs. You will learn who will be your counsellor on Orientation Day and can arrange a meeting after this. However, you may always ask for assistance at the reception desk at any time.

Accommodation
Staying with a Canadian family offers many advantages. Your Homestay hosts, arranged through the college, are people with whom you can practice your English and who will introduce you to Canadian culture. Students who wish to live on their own or with friends can find suitable accommodation through advertisements in many different publications. There are places on campus where notices are posted by students from various colleges who are looking for people to share an apartment. While looking for a suitable long-term place to stay, or requiring only short-term accommodation, students can stay at inexpensive hotels or hostels.

Medical insurance
All students must have medical insurance when they study at Pattison College. Should you wish, the College will assist you to apply for the BC Medical Services Plan, but this coverage will not take effect for three months. Students who have not arranged for medical insurance coverage before they arrive must get short term insurance costing approximately $140 for three months.

Airport pickup

Pattison College can arrange for airport pickup for students. Whether they plan to stay with a homestay host family, or have made alternative accommodation arrangements, the College will ensure that they reach their new home safely. To arrange for this service, just notify your agent or Pattison College directly.

Travel services

Students can get advice about planning trips and going on tours within the College from Canada Swan Travel. This is a travel agency affiliated with Pattison College which specializes in arranging flights for international students and tours for students wishing to visit other parts of British Columbia, Canada or the USA. They can also help you with travel arrangements by booking flights to and from your own country.

Skills practice

Section 2 vocabulary

A guided tour

1 Read the descriptions of departments, places and rooms at colleges and training centres below. Match the descriptions with the words in the box below.

a   This is an area of land containing all the main buildings of a college or university.
b   You go here to receive lessons or listen to a talk.
c   You can get information here about the costs of your course.
d   If you need somewhere to live, you should contact this department.
e   You should contact this department if you want to apply for a course.
f   This department will give you advice about finding a job.
g   You can use the computers or books in this room to study by yourself.
h   This is a place where you can buy food or drink.
i   If you have an accident at college, you should talk to someone from this department.

Self-access Centre	College Admissions	Financial Division	Lecture Room
Accommodation	Health and Safety	Careers Service	Campus Canteen

Section 2,
Reading Text 2

Remember
- Questions follow the order of the text.
- For sentence completion tasks with possible answers, you must choose an ending that fits the first part of the sentence according to meaning, not just grammar.
- You must choose answers according to information in the text.

Sentence completion (using a box of possible answers)

Look at Section 2, Reading Text 2 about fees and refunds on page 31.

Complete each sentence with the correct ending **A–I** from the box.

1   The cost of a course depends on
2   No refund will be given for
3   Students can expect to receive refunds according to
4   Confirmation of enrolment depends on
5   The amount of additional tuition fees is based on
6   There is no additional charge for

A	the examinations students may take.
B	the complete payment of every fee.
C	the language classes the college provides.
D	the number of days a student attends.
E	the number of places available.
F	the date the application is received.
G	the programme a student takes.
H	the extra credit points a student can gain.
I	the first-year enrolment fees.

Fees Policy

Students wishing to attend the college are required to pay for tuition, administration costs and materials for each year of their course. The fee is calculated according to the particular programme they intend to follow.

A NZ$175 enrolment fee is also required for international students, but this is a one-time payment for their first year only. If students decide to cancel or withdraw from a course, they may receive a refund of tuition fees but the enrolment fee is non-refundable.

Should a student wish and be entitled to claim a tuition refund, the date we receive their application is the date used to calculate the amount, rather than the last day of the student's attendance on the course. Students are advised that they should receive their refund no later than 4 weeks after the application has been submitted.

To guarantee a place on a course, students need to pay all fees in full by the deadline stated in their acceptance letter. If this condition is not met, students will not be enrolled.

In order to obtain a student permit from the immigration service, students must be studying a course which amounts to no less than 120 credit points per year, or 60 per term. Should a course the student intends to take be worth more than 120 credits, further tuition fees will be payable depending on the number of extra credit points it provides.

Students wishing to apply for pre-course English language classes should note that no fee is required. However, students will have to pay for any external examination they take in this subject.

Skills practice

Section 2 vocabulary

What's the difference?

1 Look at the pairs/groups of words below. What is the difference in meaning?

a   to apply for / to enrol on
b   costs / fees
c   to cancel / to postpone
d   to attend / to participate in
e   a condition / a rule
f   a refund / a receipt
g   a permit / permission

Sentence completion without a choice of possible answers

Look at the information about Southland College on pages 32–33.

Complete the sentences below with words taken from the passage.

Write <u>no more than three words</u> for each answer.

1 Southland College is unique because its students can gain .... during their course.
2 Applicants must have the .... necessary to do well on a course.
3 Students who have not been employed must provide the college with their ....
4 Depending on the programme, some students may have to take a test to assess their ....
5 Students should sign the contract if they agree with its ....
6 When the college receives a student's ...., it will send out a letter confirming enrolment.

Remember
- The questions follow the order of the information in the text.
- You need to write the exact words from the text.
- Read the instructions carefully: sometimes you can write up to three words or just two words. Sometimes you may need to write a number.

Section 2, Reading Text 3

Southland College of Business
INFORMATION FOR INTERNATIONAL STUDENTS

About us

Southland College of Technology is proud of its reputation as a world-class centre of learning. Our wide range of employment-related education and training courses is designed to meet the needs of the business world. As a practical part of our programmes, our students are offered valuable work experience at one of the local companies we have a connection with. It is this opportunity that makes Southland stand out from other colleges in the region.

Entry requirements

The college has established minimum entry requirements into our certificate programmes. This is to ensure that all students have the required skills and abilities to follow their course successfully. We consider that it is in the interest of all course participants that they make good progress with their studies. For all international students wishing to enroll on mainstream programmes, these requirements are:
- the student must be at least 18 years old
- the student must supply a copy of a recent IELTS or equivalent English proficiency test result (if you have not sat IELTS within the last three months, you may need to take our English placement assessment test)
- the student must supply an English transcript of their academic qualifications and/or details of relevant work experience

For certain programmes, students are required to:
- attend an interview with a course counselor and take an aptitude test to assess whether they are suitable for the chosen programme. (telephone interviews can be arranged at the expense of the applicant)

Enrolment procedure

The student should ...
- choose their proposed programme of study
- complete an international application form and send this with relevant documents

The college will ...
- consider the application and decide on the student's acceptance or rejection
- send the student an Offer of Place if the application is successful

The student should ...
- read the terms and conditions set out in the Offer of Place and if they are acceptable -
- sign the contract agreement which outlines fees and college regulations
- pay their deposit as soon as possible

The college will ...
- send confirmation of enrolment upon receipt of deposit
- send out a copy of the Student Handbook and details of the orientation programme.

Skills practice

Section 2 vocabulary

Synonyms and similar words

1 Replace an underlined word/phrase with a word/phrase from the box

job seekers   up-to-date are entitled to   criteria submit   get a discount on staff members gain entry to assignments   select designed   evaluated situated

1   Students are expected to <u>hand in</u> four <u>essays</u> during the course.
2   The college is <u>located</u> five miles from the city centre.
3   This programme is <u>suitable</u> for recent school leavers.
4   All our students <u>have the right to</u> free internet access.
5   If you are unemployed, you can <u>pay less for</u> the course.
6   Applicants must meet certain <u>requirements</u> to <u>get onto</u> a course.
7   Companies will <u>choose</u> future <u>employees</u> who have <u>the latest</u> knowledge of the market.
8   <u>People looking for work</u> can practise their interview techniques.
9   Course participants will be <u>assessed</u> on their course work as well as a final exam.

Collocation

2 Match the word on the left or right with a word in the box.

1 | further   longer | education

2 | life   living | costs

3   application | process   method |

4 | concentrated   intensive | training

5 | base   foundation | course

6   selection | course   procedure |

7   academic | demonstration   performance |

8 | work   employment | experience

Matching (people to theories/opinions, etc.)

Look at the following claims (questions **1–6**) and the list of people.

Match each claim with the person who made it.

You may use any letter more than once.

List of people

A   Dr Daniel Simons
B   Dr Edward Vogel
C   Professor Rene Marois
D   Professor Brian Butterworth

1   People's brains are more challenged now than they used to be.
2   It's possible that people with good visual memories are also clear thinkers.
3   Concentration on one subject may prevent people from noticing other details in a scene.
4   People tend to overestimate their ability to accurately remember visual details.
5   People do not always notice significant change in visual details.
6   Our poor ability to remember details may result in accidents on the road.

Remember
- In Section 3 of the reading module, you might have to do a matching task which asks you to match a list of people to findings, statements, theories or claims.
  a finding = the result of a test, research or experiment
  a statement = to make a statement is to say that something is a fact
  a theory = to have an idea about something/to say that something might be true
  a claim = to make a claim can be used for both stating a fact and expressing an opinion
- Look at the glossary to see if any important words are explained.

Section 3, Reading Text 1

Blind to details

Having trouble coping with the complexity of modern life? If so, it could be that your brain is stuck in the Stone Age, as Roger Highfield explains.

Look around and you could be forgiven for believing that you can see a vivid and detailed picture of your surroundings. Indeed, you may even think that your eyes never deceive you. [5] Unfortunately the same cannot be said for your brain. Scientists have gathered some remarkable evidence which shows that it is possible to see something without observing it, in research that sheds new light on traffic [10] accidents that occur when a driver "looked but failed to see", and other examples of our limited observation skills.

The astonishing lack of attention we pay to our surroundings has been highlighted by research [15] conducted by Dr Daniel Simons, of the University of Illinois. In one experiment, people who were walking across a college campus were asked by a stranger for directions. During the resulting conversation, [20] two men carrying a wooden door passed between the stranger and the subject*. After the door went by, the subject was asked if they had been surprised by anything. Half of those tested failed to notice that, as the door passed [25] by, a shorter, darker man was in the stranger's place. Sure enough, although the subjects had talked to the stranger for 10–15 seconds before the swap, Simons discovered that half of them were not aware that, after the passing of the [30] door, they had ended up speaking to another person.

This phenomenon highlights how we see much less than we think we do. Dr Simons came up with another demonstration based on a [35] videotape of people playing basketball. He played the tape to subjects and asked them to count the passes made by one of the teams. Around half failed to spot a woman dressed in a gorilla suit who walked slowly across the [40] scene for nine seconds, even though the 'gorilla' had passed between the players and stopped to face the camera and thump its chest. It shows, he says, that when people are really focused on something, they can be 'blind' to [45] other features in the background. However, if people were simply asked to view the tape, they noticed the gorilla easily.

Two teams have since reported complementary studies that underline our limited capacity to [50] hold a visual scene in short-term memory

(VSTM), such as a passing gorilla, revealing how our 'visual notebook' is controlled by a tiny region of the brain called the posterior parietal cortex, near the back of the head. The

55 studies were published in the journal *Nature* by Dr Edward Vogel of the University of Oregon, Eugene, and by Professor Rene Marois of Vanderbilt University, Nashville. Subjects are capable when it comes to remembering four or

60 fewer objects in a scene but are often mistaken describing displays containing more, indicating that the storage capacity of our VSTM is about four.

"Although we have the impression we are

65 taking in a great deal of information from a visual scene, we are actually very poor at describing it in detail once it is gone from our sight," said Professor Marois. In the case of the door experiment, for example, it seems that the

70 visual short-term memory capacity of the subjects meant that they did not retain enough details to spot that they were talking to a new person. According to Professor Brian Butterworth, this visual memory may also be

75 linked to intelligence. In the same way that a computer with a large working memory can tackle problems more quickly, people with a greater capacity for retaining images may be more logical and have better problem-solving

80 skills. And there may be a link with mathematical skills, notably substituting – the capacity to instantly know the exact number of objects on a screen without the need to count.

"There have been some arguments that limits

85 on visual memory are related to the number of items we can attend to at once as well as to limits on the number of items we can count at a glance (typically both have capacity estimates of around three to four)," added Dr Simons.

90 "I'm not yet convinced that the link is direct or if there are any causal relationships between these processes, but three to four does appear a lot in cognitive psychology." This research has more serious implications. This memory

95 limitation could contribute to traffic accidents, said Dr Vogel, because of the need to maintain and monitor information about other cars, pedestrians and cyclists. "While this hasn't been tested directly, it seems highly plausible

100 that racing drivers have higher VSTM capacity than normal drivers."

As far as our brains are concerned, these studies suggest that the saying 'out of sight, out of mind' may be true. Indeed, it is a

105 wonder that scientists are here to discuss the issue at all, given that the ability of our ancestors to dodge spears, clubs and pouncing lions may have been curbed by the limited capacity of human visual memory. But

110 Professor Marois said that a VSTM capacity of four was probably not much of a problem in the relatively slow-paced lives of our hunter-gatherer ancestors. But the stressful pace of modern life, he says, is stretching our Stone

115 Age brains to the limit.

Glossary
A subject: a person who takes part in an experiment/the person who is analysed/observed/interviewed, etc.

Summary with choice of possible answers

Complete the summary below using words from the box.

According to recent research into traffic accidents, a person's ability to observe what is going on around them can be quite (1) .... .In one test, people were not (2) .... that during a conversation with a stranger, someone else had taken the stranger's place. In another test, people were so (3) .... during a basketball game they didn't notice someone dressed up in a gorilla suit in the background. Further similar studies revealed how most people are only (4) .... of storing about four objects from a scene in their short-term memory. It is also thought that a person who has higher than average ability to recall visual scenes is likely to be (5) .... when it comes to solving difficult problems. However, as the average person sees and recalls four things only, this can make life in today's world seem rather (6) ....

blind	detailed	visual	stressful	remarkable	surprised
sure	focused	large	limited	mistaken	capable	aware
slow	logical

Remember
- The answers you need follow the order of the information in the text.
- See if there is a heading for the summary: this may tell you if the summary is only for part of the original article.
- Make sure the answer you choose corresponds to the information in the text and don't just use an answer that fits grammatically.
- Make sure you accurately copy the words in the box onto your answer sheet.

Global multiple choice

Choose the correct letter, **A**, **B**, **C** or **D**.

What is the writer's overall purpose in writing this article?

A to show what type of person is likely to suffer memory loss
B to encourage people to become more aware of their surroundings
C to suggest a way in which traffic accidents could be prevented
D to highlight the limits of people's memory of visual details

Skills practice

Understanding ideas

When you read a magazine, journal or newspaper article, you may not find the main topic in the first line of a paragraph. Sometimes it may be in the middle or even the end of each paragraph. For example, in the article *Blind to details*, the main topic is stated in lines 6–8: 'Scientists have gathered some remarkable evidence which shows that it is possible to see something without observing it'. It is important to recognize how the surrounding sentences relate to the main idea. You can do this by understanding:

- the meaning and function of linking words
- the way we use determiners such as : 'the' 'this' 'it' 'those', etc.
- paraphrasing: repeating the same information using different vocabulary and/or sentence structure

1 Answer the following questions about the text *Blind to details*.

1 (line 3) What is the function of *Indeed* in this context?
   (a) it shows disagreement with the previous sentence
   (b) it emphasizes the truth of the previous sentence

2 (line 5) What does *the same* mean in this sentence?

3 (lines 13–14) *The astonishing lack of attention we pay to our surroundings* is a paraphrase of which sentence in paragraph 1?

4 (lines 23–24) What three words could you add to *Half of those ....* *tested…*?

5 (line 26) What linking words could replace the word *although*?

6 (line 32) What does *This phenomenon* refer to?

7 (line 43) What does *It* refer to?

8 (line 45) What is the function of *However* in this context?
   (a) it is followed by a comparison.
   (b) it is followed by a disagreement.

Classification

Classify the points in the article about salt.

Write

A if the writer presents the point as a fact
B if the writer presents the point as a possibility
C if the writer doesn't mention the point

1 there is no good reason for children to be on a low-salt diet
2 some companies have deliberately misled people about the effects of salt
3 a lack of iodine is dangerous for pregnant women
4 salt use has been decreasing since the 1990s in New Zealand

<table>
<tr><td>

Remember
- Classification tasks do not follow the order of information in the text.
- Remember that you do not need to understand every word in the article: read the questions below first so you know the kind of information you are looking for.

</td></tr>
</table>

5   a health campaign has led to illness amongst New Zealand children
6   an increase of potassium in the diet is more significant than a reduction in salt
7   the health benefits of salt depend on the way it has been refined
8   children in New Zealand are not getting enough iodine nowadays

Multiple matching

Choose **FOUR** letters from the list **A–H** below.

Which four general uses of salt below are mentioned in the article?

A a way of preventing infections
B a safety measure on roads
C a supplement to the diet of animals
D a way of keeping food fresh
E a means of payment
F a means of softening water
G a flavouring
H a stage of an industrial process

Global

Choose the correct letter, **A**, **B**, **C** or **D**.

Which of the following is the most suitable title for the passage on pages 37–38?

A The importance of reducing salt
B Salt use around the globe
C Marketing the benefits of salt
D The role of salt in a healthy diet

Section 3, Reading Text 2

"Pass the salt" used to be a routine request at every meal time but over the past decades, salt has been under attack from the health establishment. The campaign against salt has been so successful that New Zealand is now experiencing an epidemic of goitre, an enlargement of the thyroid gland which causes swelling in the throat, usually found in much poorer countries. One of the causes of goitre is iodine* deficiency and, since New Zealand soils are naturally low in that element, iodine has been added to table salt since the 1920's. Avoid table salt and you risk missing out on this essential micronutrient. In pregnant women, iodine deficiency can cause serious harm to the baby's health. A study of 300 eight to ten year old New Zealand children in the late 1990s found that 11.3% showed signs of iodine deficiency, having thyroids greater in size than the upper limit for their ages. An incidence of goitre greater than 5% is considered an epidemic.

Some people use only 'natural' dirty salts, which they imagine are better for you than factory-refined white salt, just as wholemeal bread is deemed to be more healthful than refined white bread. In fact, supermarket salt is a great deal healthier, since it contains the iodine that people may not be getting elsewhere. The study found that about one-third of the children's care givers did not use iodised salt in cooking and about half the children did not used iodised salt at the table. The children were studied in the late 90s, so it's probable that salt use has declined even more since then.

Leaving aside the issue of iodine deficiency, salt is essential for human health. If totally deprived of salt you will die, and a salt deficiency causes headaches and weaknesses, lightheadedness, then nausea. Normally, though, salt deficiency is rare, even on a low-salt diet, because salt is added to everything from bread to baked beans, for taste or to aid preservation or both. The sodium* in salt, if not flushed out of your body by your kidneys, will increase the amount of fluid in your blood and cause your heart to work harder, putting extra pressure on your arterial walls. If you're young and don't suffer from hypertension, there's not much evidence to support a low-salt diet, and there seems no case at all for restricting the table salt intake of children, except perhaps to get them accustomed to a low-salt diet that might benefit them in middle age.

There has always been considerable scientific debate about how much benefit we derive from reducing our salt intake. In 1984, the famous Intersalt study was supposed to settle the matter. The study was huge: it encompassed 200 individuals, both male and female aged 20 to 60 in 52 communities across the world. The communities ranged from those with the lowest to the highest salt intake. It compared blood pressure and salt consumption. Of the 52 communities, 48 showed no relationship between sodium intake and blood pressure. In fact, the community in Tianjin, China, which had the highest salt intake – 14g a day — had the median blood pressure of 119/70, about the same as the group with the lowest intake of six grams. There now seems to be a consensus that salt reduction does have a positive effect on blood pressure, although there is still disagreement about how great that effect is. However, a 1997 study called DASH (Dietary Approaches to Stop Hypertension) – demonstrated that a potassium*-rich diet of fruit, vegetables, whole grains, nuts and low-fat dairy products substantially reduced blood pressure, even when salt intake remained the same. A second study showed that a DASH diet combined with low sodium intake reduced blood pressure even further.

Removing salt from the table, then, is not going to be enough to improve our health and it would be a shame if it disappeared from the dinner table. Salt has had a unique and enduring place in human history and has helped shape civilization. It was once one of the most sought after and valuable substances on the planet. Without it, long journeys became impossible and armies were unable to wage war. Soldiers often died from minor wounds because there was no salt for disinfectants. In Roman times, soldiers were sometimes paid in salt, hence the origin of the word 'salary'. In the US, many secondary roads were originally trails made by animals searching for salt. Like humans, animals need salt and seek out brine springs or rock salt, which they lick. Farmers must provide their livestock with salt when they cannot seek it out for themselves. The quest for salt inspired technology that changed our world: it was the drilling techniques developed by salt prospectors, for example, that led to the discovery of oil reserves. Oil and gas are frequently found close to salt deposits. So – pass the salt!

Glossary
Iodine/sodium/potassium : these are all chemical elements.

Skills practice

Recognizing the writer's attitude

In the article about salt, we can understand that the writer believes that the balanced use of salt is a good thing from the language he uses:

salt has been heavily attacked

avoid table salt and you risk missing out on this essential micronutrient.

it would be a shame if it disappeared from the dinner table.

We can also understand a writer's intention from verbs or nouns which express attitude.

What attitude is shown in each sentence below?

A Write **a** for approval or **b** for disapproval.

B Write **a** for strong possibility or **b** for doubt.

C Write **a** for expectation or **b** for surprise.

A

It's time that we
It would be no bad thing if the government } banned smoking in public places

I am in full agreement with the proposal
It hardly seems fair } to ban smoking in public places

I am against
I object to
We must back
I feel we should resist
It's my belief that we should make a stand against
I am strongly opposed to
I am in favour of } the banning of smoking in public places

B

It hardly seems likely that
In all likelihood,
There is little doubt that
It's doubtful whether
It is questionable whether
One has to be sceptical about whether
In all probability,
It's fairly certain that } mankind will be living on other planets in the 21st century

C

Predictably, they found that
It came as no surprise to find that
In fact, they found that
Indeed, they found that
They could not have foreseen that
Just as they had anticipated,
They actually found that } the product was harmful

YES/NO/NOT GIVEN

Do the following statements agree with the claims of the writer of the passage on pages 40–41?

Write:

YES if the statement agrees with the claims of the writer.
NO if the statement contradicts the claims of the writer.
NOT GIVEN if it is impossible to say what the writer thinks.

1 Parents today are not surprised when their children return home.
2 American children who return home have respect for their parents.
3 Men and women may share the same reasons for returning home.
4 Parents expect children who return home to make a financial contribution.
5 The suggestions that Mary Bold makes should work well for most families.
6 Dave Hendl blames himself for his son's lack of independence.
7 Young people nowadays believe it should be unnecessary to work as hard as their parents did.

Locating information

Section 3, Reading Text 3 on pages 40–41 has seven paragraphs labelled **A–G**.

Which paragraph contains the following information?

1 the idea of mature or immature behaviour not depending on age.
2 the idea of young people returning home being a historical one.
3 an explanation that supports the behaviour of children who do not leave home.
4 the fact that young people enjoy spending their money on what they want.
5 evidence that the modern trend of children returning home is not limited to one culture.

Global

In this **article**, the writer is

A condemning children for their materialistic attitude.
B criticizing parents for their poor child-raising skills.
C expressing regret for loss of traditional relationships.
D illustrating a trend concerning living arrangements.

Section 3, Reading Text 3

Crowded House

A
There are a number of cultures which share a similar fable; that of the ambitious child who leaves home and then suddenly returns, a failure. The astonished parents are simply relieved they are safe and back home. In the modern take on this theme, sure, the parents would also celebrate, wash the child's socks and kindly commiserate but they would hardly find it remarkable when their kids turned up on the doorstep having squandered the job, the flat, the partner and the loan. The return of grown children to the family house has become commonplace. But each time they come back, the welcomes must become less enthusiastic, as parents, all prepared for an empty-nest, find instead that their chicks have grown in size, but never properly leave.

B
Who says you can never go back? Everybody's doing it. There are even national derogatory names for the species: 'boomerang children' or 'boomerangs' in English-speaking countries are 'parasite singles' in Japan and 'mama's boys' in Italy. Figures from the US suggest that 18 million Americans aged 18–34 live with their parents –about one third of the age group. Of this lot, 4.5 million are over 25. UK statistics show the same pattern; two surveys last year showed that the proportion of young adults who return home after

initially leaving has nearly doubled since the late 1950s, from 25% to 46% – and also provided the shameful statistic that 10% of 35–44 year olds still get mum to do their washing.

C

In the case of women, Canterbury University psychologist Dr Mark Byrd says that they might be seeking safe-harbour. "This tends to happen when they get married, have kids, get a divorce, and find they can't live on their own and their parents are there to provide shelter and a baby-sitting service." For men, he says, it's less socially acceptable. For a man, the return to cooked meals, a laundry service and maternal love is regarded as a refusal to grow up. However, by no means is this reluctance only a masculine trait. Other theories blame materialism and a lack of maturity among the pampered young. The ever-receding average marriage age might be the reason why so many singles are sitting at home, but consumerism appears to compensate amply for their lack of a spouse. Back in the family home, they have the option to treat nearly all of their earnings as disposable income.

D

In the family-based societies there is no stigma attached to such parasitism. But in countries where flat-sharing is still seen as the norm, this behaviour is derided, seen as some kind of independence aversion, and a reluctance to grow up. *Boomerang Kids*, by Mary Bold, PhD, purports to show how you can avoid having a perpetual adolescent in the house. She insists there are various conditions to 'make a re-filled nest work well'. Some of these seem straightforward, if not necessarily easy; others impossible to monitor and enforce. According to Bold, 'boomerangers' must pay rent , they need to get along with mum, they can only return once, their return must be regarded as a safety net only, they must be good company. In real life, no-one is that structured. 'Boomerangs' told me their families made it up as they went along, with mostly satisfactory results. But satisfactory for whom?

E

For example, Simon, a 30-year-old lawyer, says his mother does everything. "It's like living in a hotel. There's no expectation that I have to contribute at all." Dr Byrd is not impressed by scenarios like these, which he says leads to social retardation. "You have to agree that you're all adults living together,' he says. "If the parents still treat the young adult as a child, that's harmful for the development of the child and the parents as well." When does one become an adult? Byrd says "Age boundaries are not numbers. In public, people might be treated as adults, might be adults, but, at home all of a sudden you're treated and you might act as though you're fourteen. Then it's not so much about age boundaries as about your attitude towards those you interact with."

F

Dave and Wendy Hendl are in their sixties. Their second-youngest child, Joe, is 26 and still at home. "We thought we'd have an empty nest by now," says Dave. "But it doesn't concern us." He admits things are occasionally difficult because 'Joe's trying to mark out his own space'. Generously, he suggests that his children might take a while to get used to taking on adult responsibilities, "but they're probably exposed to more of life earlier." And guess what? It's all down to the parents. "We probably should have forced responsibility on to the kids and made them more aware of the value of looking after themselves."

G

Most commentators are content to mock 'boomerangs' as overgrown infants, but their decision to trade impoverished independence for higher purchasing power has a certain depressing rationality. Children of middle-class baby boomers* know that the world owes them nothing – their parents' generation has seen to that. They expect to struggle for the milestones that former generations took for granted – a degree, a career path, a house, a pension. At the same time, they want immediate job fulfillment and a satisfying social life. So it makes sense to exact a sort of retribution by continuing to be a burden on the family. This contradiction between continued dependence and the desire for autonomy might seem adolescent. But perhaps that's the point. Boomerang kids' unwillingness to leave adolescence mirrors the baby boomers' increasingly frantic attempts to stay young.

Glossary
*baby boomers = people born between the mid 1940's to 1960's in the West
spouse = a formal term for either a husband or wife

Skills practice

Understanding the writer's purpose

In some of the general multiple-choice questions in Section 3 (eg Choose **A**, **B**, **C** or **D**) or in the global purpose multiple-choice question, you may be asked to identify the writer's purpose or intention.

example: What is the writer's purpose in writing this article?

A to **encourage** people to eat more healthily
B to **highlight** the causes of poor health
C to **emphasize** the risks of over-exercising
D to **suggest** other means of keeping fit

1 Look at the groups of words/phrases below. For each line, choose a word/phrase which does **not** have the same meaning as the others. Use a dictionary to help you.

a to describe/to highlight/to emphasize/to underline
b to illustrate/to exemplify/to demonstrate/to discuss
c to express disapproval of/to criticize/to condemn/to contrast
d to suggest/to summarize/to propose/to recommend
e to evaluate/to analyse/to introduce/to assess

Section 3, Reading Text 4

Remember
- Multiple-choice questions follow the order of the text.
- Read the question carefully: more than one of the answers may seem correct but only one will fit the question exactly.

Multiple choice

Look at Section 3, Reading Text 4 about clever canines on pages 44–45.

Questions **1–5**

Choose the correct letter **A**, **B**, **C** or **D**.

1 According to Csányi, dogs have similar patterns of behaviour to people because they
A share the same basic need to belong to a group.
B were one of the first species to be trained.
C have become dependent on humans for survival.
D have adapted to a human environment.

2 In paragraph 2, what are we told about barking as a means of communication?
A Dogs do not have the emotional range that many people think they do.
B People who are not dog owners can often understand what dogs mean.
C The number and type of barks that dogs use has increased over time.
D People can clearly recognize barks that indicate the dog has met a stranger.

3 What conclusions did Csányi reach after comparing dogs to wolves?
A An action needs to be seen many times before a dog can understand it.
B Domesticated dogs require permission before they will perform an action.
C Dogs that are pets have lost the abilities that other dogs still possess.
D Wolves probably have less intellectual ability than dogs.

4 What point does the writer make about chimpanzees and dogs?
A Dogs are able to concentrate on a task longer than a chimpanzee.
B Chimpanzees are less willing to be trained than dogs are.
C Unlike chimpanzees, dogs know when a person is unaware of something.
D Experiments that involve food will work better with dogs than chimpanzees.

5 What point is made by the reference to the 'Clever Hans effect'?
A Researchers do not always consider what can influence an experiment.
B Domesticated animals can often form a strong connection with one person.
C What science has accepted as fact may often be proved to be wrong later.
D It is easy to deceive people who want to believe animals have special talents.

Summary (without answers)

Questions **6–11**

Complete the summary below.

Choose no more than **THREE WORDS** from the passage on pages 44–45 for each answer.

The argument against Csányi's theories

Michael J Owren doubts that dogs possess the (6) .... that Csányi believes. He thinks the dogs simply make a connection between (7) .... , rather than actually think about a situation or process. According to Owren, dogs are able to observe certain (8) .... that humans give and this is the reason for their successful (9) ....

Raymond P. Coppinger also doubts Csányi's findings . He points out that the dogs he used in the experiment belong to the (10) .... This particular group of dogs can manage a variety of (11) .... because of the way they have been bred, so we cannot compare their abilities with dogs in general.

Questions **12–13**

Choose **TWO** letters **A–E**

Which two of the following abilities did Csányi test in dogs ?
A The ability to remember people from previous occasions.
B The ability to obtain food that is difficult to reach.
C The ability to locate hidden toys.
D The ability to copy human movement.
E The ability to open a barrier.

Skills practice

How punctuation helps you understand meaning

Look at the following examples of punctuation. How do they affect the meaning of the surrounding text?

1 What does the colon (:) tell us in these sentences?
a Vilmos Csányi's department is full of canines: dogs are in the hall, in the classroom and working in the laboratories …
b Chimpanzees … do very poorly in the following classic experiment: a researcher hides food in one of several containers out of sight of the animal – then the chimp is allowed to choose one container after the experimenter indicates the correct choice
c Those results left researchers with a question: if dogs can pick up on human cues, do they put out cues for humans to understand?

2 What do the inverted commas (' ... ') tell us in this sentence?
Hans was clever enough to figure out that he would get a treat if he stopped tapping when the human in front of him reacted to the arrival of the 'correct answer'

3 What is the purpose of the semi-colon (;) in the example below?
What other punctuation could replace it?
Hans was clever enough to figure out that he would get a treat if he stopped tapping when the human in front of him subtly reacted to the arrival of the 'correct answer'; the horse didn't actually know arithmetic.

4 What information are we given after the commas (,) in these sentences?
a There are no cages at Loránd Eötvös University's department of ethology, the study of animal behavior.
b He recruited 90 human volunteers and played them 21 recordings of barking Hungarian mudis, a breed of dog that herd sheep.

Clever Canines

Did domestication make dogs smarter?

Vilmos Csányi's department is full of canines: dogs are in the hall, in the classroom and working in the laboratories where Mr. Csányi and his colleagues are trying to determine just how much their brains are capable of. There are no cages at Loránd Eötvös University's department of ethology, the study of animal behavior. And why would there be? asks Mr. Csányi, the department's founder and chairman. In adjusting to our world, Mr. Csányi argues, our best friends have acquired a remarkable number of mental characteristics that closely resemble our own. His team has been studying canine cognition* for the past decade and has evidence that suggests dogs have far greater mental capabilities than scientists have previously believed. "Our experiments indicate a high level of social understanding in dogs," he says. And in their relationship with humans, dogs have developed remarkable interspecies-communications skills. "They easily accept a membership in the family, they provide and request information, and are able to cooperate and imitate human actions," he says.

The latest findings to come out of the department suggest that dogs' barks have evolved into a relatively sophisticated way of communicating with humans. Adam Miklósi, an ethology professor, set out to see if humans can interpret what dogs mean when they bark. He recruited 90 human volunteers and played them 21 recordings of barking Hungarian mudis, a breed* of dog that herd sheep. The recordings captured dogs in seven situations, such as playing with other dogs, anticipating food, and encountering a human intruder. The people showed strong agreement about the emotional meaning of the various barks, regardless of whether they owned a mudi or another breed, or had never owned a dog. Owners and nonowners were also just as successful at deducing the situation that had elicited the barks, guessing correctly in a third of the situations, or about double the rate of chance.

In scientific circles, animal-cognition studies have focused on animals such as chimpanzees. And until recently, dogs were also thought to be intellectually inferior to wolves. A study published in 1985 by Harry Frank, a psychologist at the University of Michigan, showed that wolves could unlock a complicated gate mechanism after watching a human do it once, while dogs remained confused, even after considerable exposure. This led some scientists to conclude that dogs' intellectual capacity diminished during domestication*. But Csányi suspected that dogs were simply more inhibited than their wild cousins, requiring a signal from their masters before opening a gate. So eight years ago, he conducted a problem-solving experiment of his own. With their masters present, 28 dogs of various ages, breeds, and levels of training had to figure out how to pull on handles of plastic dishes to obtain meat on the other side of a wire fence. Regardless of other factors, the dogs with the strongest relationship with their owner scored worst, continually seeking approval or assistance. The best results came from outdoor dogs, who obtained the meat, on average, in one-third the time. Most telling, when owners were allowed to signal approval, the gap between indoor and outdoor dogs vanished.

That made the researchers wonder what else the dogs could achieve by taking cues from people. Chimpanzees have been shown to follow a human's gaze, but they do very poorly in the following classic experiment: a researcher hides food in one of several containers out of sight of the animal – then the chimp is allowed to choose one container after the experimenter indicates the correct choice by various methods, such as staring, nodding, pointing and so on. Only with considerable training do chimpanzees manage to score above chance. Dogs, however, performed marvelously. By 2001 experiments by Mr. Csányi's team showed that dogs were far more skilled than chimps at using human social cues* to find food. Those results left researchers with a question: if dogs can pick up on human cues, do they put out cues for humans to understand?

To find out, Mr. Csányi went to the homes of Budapest's many dog owners. After introducing the researchers to the dogs, the owners would leave the room. Then the dogs would watch Mr. Csányi hide a piece of food somewhere inaccessible to them. When the owners returned, the dogs would run or glance back and forth from master to hiding place, clearly signaling its location. More recent experiments substituted nonfood objects and had similar results, which suggests the dogs may be placing themselves in their owner's shoes, and realizing that the humans are ignorant of the object's location. Similar testing on chimpanzees has not found evidence of the same skill.

Not everyone agrees with their findings. Raymond P. Coppinger, a dog cognition specialist, is concerned that researchers like Csányi are failing to properly control experiments for the "Clever Hans effect," named after a horse that tapped out the answers to mathematical problems more than a century ago. Although people at the time were amazed at Hans' ability, scientists later concluded that the horse was picking up unintentional cues from the person who posed the question. Hans was clever enough to figure out that he would get a treat if he stopped tapping when the human in front of him subtly reacted to the arrival of the 'correct answer'; the horse didn't actually know arithmetic.

And Michael J. Owren, assistant professor of psychology at Cornell University, will also not go so far as the Hungarians in crediting dogs with relatively high cognitive skills. He says Mr. Csányi's team may be underestimating the flexibility of associative learning, the most basic kind of learning that comes not from "thinking" out the problem, but simply by associating events or objects with one another. "Dogs are supremely sensitive to cues being produced by humans and are able to interact with humans very effectively," Mr. Owren says. "Csányi's team are using pet-class dogs who have been socialized in a very unique way," adds Coppinger. "To be talking about dogs in general when you are only referring to this small population which have been bred for all sorts of specific tasks is going to mislead us about what dogs can do or how they evolved."

Glossary
cognition = knowledge/ the process of gaining knowledge
breed = a class or type of animal, for example :
  dogs = Labrador, German Shepherd
  cats = Siamese, Burmese
domestication = the process of making animals live with or work for humans
cues = signals

Study Skills: Writing

How much do you know about the IELTS General Training Writing module?

Do the quiz below to find out.

Writing Task 1

In Task 1 you will be asked to write a transactional letter, for example, a letter asking for or providing information, expressing your opinion or making suggestions.

Skills development

1 Read the three tasks **A, B** and **C**. Which task(s) requires you to:

> write a letter of complaint   make an invitation   give factual information
> give your opinion about a general problem   make recommendations

2 Which task(s) requires you to write a formal, semi-formal or informal letter?

A

You have read in your local newspaper that there has been an increase in the amount of crime committed by young people.
Write a letter to the newspaper. In your letter

- *explain what crimes are common in your area*
- *say why you think young people are committing these crimes*
- *suggest what you think should be done about this problem*

Write at least 150 words.

Begin your letter as follows:

To the Editor,

Remember

- Think about who you are writing to. You should use informal language if you are writing to a friend and more formal language to people you don't know.
- Answer all three points in the task.
- If possible, use your own vocabulary and not the vocabulary you see in the task.
- Use a different paragraph for each point.
- You should spend about 20 minutes on Task 1. Task 1 is worth 1/3 of the marks in the Writing test.
- Don't write your address.
- Don't write less than 150 words.
- Make sure you finish the letter – for example: *from Anna* (informal letter) *Yours faithfully, Anna Taylor* (formal letter)

B

You have just returned from a two week holiday in an English-speaking friend's home. You want to thank him/her.
Write a letter to your friend. In your letter
- *say what you enjoyed about your holiday*
- *mention a problem you had during your journey home*
- *invite your friend to stay with you*

Write at least 150 words.

Begin your letter as follows:

Dear

C

There have recently been some problems with public transport in your area.
Write a letter to the manager of the local transport authority. In your letter
- *explain what these problems are*
- *say how these problems are affecting local people*
- *say what changes could be made*

Write at least 150 words.

Begin your letter:

Dear Sir or Madam,

Skills practice

Language focus

1 *Opening lines for formal or semi-formal letters*

In **Task A** page 46, you are writing a formal letter to the editor of a newspaper. You could start the letter like this:

To the editor,

I am writing in response to your recent article on crime.

You can use the same basic structure whenever you have read an article in a newspaper or magazine and want to give your opinion, for example:

I am writing   in response to   your recent advertisement for
your request for
your story about

Look at the other opening lines below. Choose a phrase from the box to express the writer's attitude about a situation/problem/something he/she has read.

| surprise at   inform about |
| gratitude for |
| concern about |
| anger about |
| dissatisfaction with |

a   I am writing to express my … (I'm worried about the situation)
b   I am writing to express my … (I'm angry about the situation)
c   I am writing to express my … (I want to thank you/someone)
d   I am writing to express my … (I'm disappointed/ I expected better)
e   I am writing to express my … (I expected something different)
f   I am writing to … you … (I want to tell you something)

Read the opening lines below. What is the purpose of each letter?

g   Dear Sir/Madam,
    I recently stayed at your hotel, from 9th–13th December. **Unfortunately,** we experienced a number of problems with our room.

h   Dear Sir/Madam,
    I am writing to **enquire about** the facilities in your conference centre.

i   Dear Sir/Madam,
    I am writing to **apologize for** the late arrival of your order.

2 *Endings for formal or semi-formal letters*

Read the endings below. Choose the type of letter (i or ii) that they would be suitable for.

a   Thank you for your assistance / attention.
   i   a letter asking for help or information
   ii a reply to a letter of enquiry

b   Once again, we apologize for any inconvenience.
   i   a letter asking for help or information
   ii a letter saying sorry about a problem or situation

c   Please do not hesitate to contact us if you require further information.
   i   a reply to a letter of enquiry
   ii a letter to a newspaper about a local situation

d   I hope you will take these points into consideration.
   i   a letter explaining some problems / suggesting solutions
   ii a letter describing the writer's skills and qualifications

e   I hope you will soon take steps to solve this problem.
   i   a letter which described problems
   ii a letter which offered solutions

f   I hope to receive your prompt answer and a refund.
   i   a letter to a newspaper about a local situation
   ii a letter of complaint

g   I hope something is done about this situation before too long.
   i   a reply to a letter of enquiry a letter
   ii a letter to a newspaper about a local issue

3 *Openings for informal/friendly letters*

In **Task B** page 47 you are writing an informal letter to a friend. You could start the letter like this:

Dear Paul,
This is just a quick letter to say thank you for my holiday.

You can use the same basic structure whenever you are writing a short letter or note, for example:

This is just a	short	letter	to	explain what/how/why ...
	quick	note		say thank you for ...
				invite you to ...
				say sorry for ...
	brief	email		ask you ...
				tell you ...
				remind you ...

Look at the other opening lines below. <u>Underline</u> the words **in bold** which are correct.

a It's been	**ages**	since	*we met us.*
	recently		*I heard from you.*
	a while		*we saw each other.*
	a long time		*I wrote to you.*

b How are you? How's everything	**doing?**
	going?
	getting?

	doing		family?
c How are you? How are you	going	on with your	new job? training course?
	getting		studies?

Remember
- We use the verb 'hope' when something is possible:
  I hope you feel better.
  I hope you can come to the party.
  I hope you get the job.
- We use the verb 'wish' when something is not possible or not true.
  I wish I could come to the party! (but I can't)
  I wish I spoke Spanish! (but I don't)
  I wish I had studied for this test! (but I didn't)

4 Endings for informal letters

Match an ending to the type of letter it would be suitable for.

Ending	The type of letter
a I hope you feel better soon!	I a letter introducing the writer
b Give me a call and let me know what you think.	II a letter giving advice
c I hope you sort things out soon.	III a letter offering sympathy
d I'm looking forward to meeting you.	IV a letter suggesting a plan/idea

Complete these final sentences with one word.

e .... my love/regards/best wishes to your family.

f .... a great time/weekend/birthday!

g .... again for the fantastic present/ your help/ letting me borrow the car.

5 Making suggestions

You may need to make suggestions for both Task 1 and Task 2. We often use the modal verbs 'should' and 'could' to make suggestions in both formal and informal writing.

Rewrite the sentences below so that they are *more* formal.

a If we want to reduce traffic jams, the council should build more roads in this area.
   I recommend ....

b The council should also provide more buses.
   Another possibility ....

c To help the environment, we could recycle our paper and glass.
   To help the environment, one idea would ....

d School children should study practical subjects so they can find jobs more easily.
   If school children .... practical subjects, they .... jobs more easily.

e In order to be healthy, we should eat a balanced diet.
   In order to be healthy, the first step ....

f If you want to reduce the amount of litter, you should provide more litter bins.
   I suggest .... more litter bins if you want to reduce the amount of litter.

Rewrite the sentences below so they are more *in*formal.

g You should try yoga if you have a bad back.
   Why don't .... if you have a bad back?

h If you want somewhere to stay, you could stay with me.
   If you want somewhere to stay, how about .... with me?

6 *Formal and informal language*

Read **Task A** on page 46 again. Then read the answer below. <u>Underline</u> the phrases which are formal and suitable for this letter.

To the editor,

I am writing in response to your recent article on crime. In Northbridge, there has also been a **considerable/big** rise in the number of burglaries. **In fact/Actually,** last week, three houses in the street where I live were broken into and **someone took valuable jewelry/valuable jewelry was taken.** The growing amount of vandalism that **can be seen/you can see** in the town centre is also shocking.

I am certain that this rise is **because of/due to** the fact that unemployment is **extremely/really** high in this area, especially among young people. People who have been unemployed for **ages/a long time** often become desperate, and young people often feel pressurized into following their friends' behaviour, even if it is criminal.

If the local council offered free training courses for the unemployed, it might help them to find jobs/The local council must offer free training courses for the unemployed so they can find jobs and stay away from trouble. Young people need to have self-respect before they can respect other people in society.

I want something to be done/I hope something is done about this situation before too long.

Yours sincerely

Jamie Felton

---

7 *Find the mistake*

Read **Task B** on page 47 again. Then read the answer below. There is one vocabulary or grammar mistake in every line. Find the mistakes and make corrections.

Dear Alex,

This is just a short letter to say thank you so much for invite me to your home.   1

I had really a great time. I think you live in an incredibly beautiful country!   2

Especially, I loved our trip in the mountains, even though I was exhausted!   3

On the way home, I had a ten hours wait at Los Angeles airport because of bad   4

weather. I was really annoying and I spent the rest of my money on lots of cups   5

of coffee. I can't tell you how happy was I to finally get home.   6

Anyway, I would really like you to come to New York next year. It is plenty of   7

room in my apartment so you could stay here as long time as you like. We could   8

spend a day wandering round Central Park, see a baseball game — whatever do you   9

like. It's also worth to spend a whole day at least in the Metropolitan Museum.   10

Get in touch and let me know what you are thinking.   11

Thanks again,

Andy

8 *Looking at students' answers*

Examiners use nine bands to assess students' writing ability. Band 1 is the lowest band.

Band 9 is the highest.

For Task 1, students need to show their ability in the following areas:

TASK ACHIEVEMENT	Are all three points answered clearly and fully in the letter?
COHERENCE AND COHESION	Is the letter well organized? Does it make sense? Is there a logical connection between clauses, sentences or ideas?
LEXICAL RESOURCE	Is there a good range of vocabulary in the letter? Is the vocabulary suitable for a formal, semi-formal or informal letter?
GRAMMATICAL RANGE AND ACCURACY	Is there a good range of grammatical structures? Is the grammar correct or are there many mistakes?

Read **Task C** on page 47 again. Then read the two answers below and make notes in the tables underneath.

Sample answer 1:

Dear Sir or Madam

Yesterday was my moving day from homestay to new flat. I waited for a bus for over one hours. I was angly. So I told friends about this story. But they have also experienced this kind of problem. As a result I would like to talk to you about some problem with public transport in my area.

First, buses never come to on time. so people have to usually wait for a bus for a long time. If we have an important appointment or meeting. we will be affraid of waiting bus. Of course we can use other transport, but it is also not easy to use. Second, sometimes they don't have any coin for change, so one day I had only $20 paper, but the driver didn't have any coin, so I was very embarssed. Fortunatly, one passenger helped me. So I could get on the bus. But I can't imagine if no-one helped me.

These problems are not just for me. Most people feel same to me. We fed up waiting for buses. It is difficult to meet friend on time. And we always prepared coin for bus fare. It is very annoyed. So, please you would solve these problem.

Sooyeon Bae

---

202 words

TASK ACHIEVEMENT	COHERENCE AND COHESION	LEXICAL RESOURCE	GRAMMATICAL RANGE AND ACCURACY

Sample answer 2:

Dear Sir or Madam

I normally take a bus to town centre because it is cheap, convenient and I can take a rest on bus.

However, a few problems of bus should be improved. The crucial part is timetable because buses in this area aren't always punctual. If I had an important appointment and had to go to town centre, I would take a bus. But the timetable of buses often changes so I don't know what time buses will arrive and departure. Buses are usually late or leave earlier.

Because of this problem, I have to drive. I must set out earlier than usual to find a parking space but there are insufficient in car parks. I spend my time and money to pay a parking ticket. It costs £1 an hour.

I know it is difficult to build a new car park so I have a suggestion to solve buses' problem. If buses were reliable and certain timetable every day, people know they could attent their meetings on time. They could not only save time but also money. I believe that residents would be happier than now.

Thank you very much for reading.

Your sincerely

Angeline

TASK ACHIEVEMENT	COHERENCE AND COHESION	LEXICAL RESOURCE	GRAMMATICAL RANGE AND ACCURACY

Skills development

Understanding the instructions and the question

IELTS General Training Writing Task 2 questions usually include the following statements:

- You should spend about 40 minutes on this task.
- Write about the following topic:
- Give reasons for your answer and include any relevant examples from your own knowledge or experience.

1 Decide if these statements are True or False.

A You must spend exactly 40 minutes on this task.
B To write about the topics, you need general rather than specialist knowledge.
C You don't need to include your opinions.
D You should present a clear argument and give some examples and reasons.
E Your writing should be in an informal, personal style.

Writing Task 2 questions usually include one of these instructions:

I   Is this true in your country?
II   Discuss both of these views and give your own opinions.
III What do you think are the causes of this problem/and how should it be solved?

IV   What is your opinion about this?
V   What is the situation in your country?
VI   Why is this the case? What can be done about this problem?
VII   Do you agree or disagree?
VIII What do you think are the advantages and disadvantages of this?

2 Which two instructions above ask you (mainly) to ...

A give only your personal views?
B show two sides of an argument?
C explain why something has happened?
D describe or compare your country to the country/countries in the opening statement?
E suggest solutions?

> **Remember**
> You can include your personal opinion in any Task 2 answer. However, your style of writing should still be semi-formal to formal.

Understanding the topic and the task

Read the essay question. Answer these questions.

Some people believe that television has brought many benefits to people's lives. Others believe that it has had a negative effect. Discuss both of these views and give your own opinions.

1 What is the main topic?
A How the TV has been replaced by other media
B How people are influenced by TV

C Television in different countries

2 What is the task?
A Suggest ways to encourage people to be more active
B Describe the kind of programmes in your country
C Give reasons + examples why watching TV can be good or bad for people

Skills practice

1 Identify the topic and analyse the tasks for these questions.

> Write about the following topic:
>
> *In the past people often got married and had children when they were very young. Nowadays many people choose to start a family later on in life.*
> *What do you think are the advantages and disadvantages of this development?*
>
> Give reasons for your answer and include any relevant examples from your own knowledge or experience.

Main topic:
Task: Do you need to ...
    ... focus more on the present situation than the past?
        YES/NO
    ... include the good and bad points about having children when you're older?
        YES/NO
    ... suggest ways that people with children can be helped by the government?
        YES/NO

> **Remember**
> • You must write at least the number of words given or you will lose marks.
> • You will not have time to count words in the exam, so count words when you are practising so you know roughly how much to write.

> Write about the following topic:
>
> *People who live and work in large cities often complain that they are suffering from stress.*
> *What do you think are the causes of this problem and how should it be solved?*
>
> Give reasons for your answer and include any relevant examples from your own knowledge or experience.

Main topic:
Task: Do you need to …

… suggest ways that stress could be reduced?	YES/NO
… give examples of what might cause people's stress?	YES/NO
… compare life in the city to life in the countryside?	YES/NO

> Write about the following topic:
>
> *In Britain, many traditions and customs are changing or have disappeared completely.*
> *What is the situation in your country?*
>
> Give reasons for your answer and include any relevant examples from your own knowledge or experience.

Main topic:
Task: Do you need to …

… describe some of the customs and traditions in your country ?	YES/NO
… compare your country to Britain?	YES/NO
… discuss the advantages and disadvantages of keeping traditions?	YES/NO

Writing style in Task 2 essays

For Task 2, you often need to present your opinion about an issue, discuss advantages and disadvantages, or show two different points of view.

Look at the statements below about argumentative essay writing in English. Underline the word/phrase **in bold** which you think is true for English native speakers.

English native speakers …

1   … write the main purpose of the essay in the **first paragraph/final paragraph.**
2   … write about different topics in **the same/separate** paragraphs.
3   … usually write paragraphs which are **about two lines/more than two lines.**
4   … are usually **indirect and suggestive/direct and assertive** when they make a claim.
5   … make a claim and give one or more **factual examples/several anecdotes.**
6   … **often/rarely** mention their own point of view in the opening paragraph.
7   … normally use **short/long** sentences in this kind of writing.

Brainstorming and planning

1 Look at the question about the effect of television on people's lives. Then decide where to put the notes in the table. The first one has been done for you as an example.

Some people believe that television has brought many benefits to people's lives. Others believe that it has had a negative effect. Discuss both of these views and give your own opinions.

Remember
- It is difficult to write an organized essay if you are thinking about language structures and ideas for your answer at the same time.
- Make a list of ideas first.
- Decide on the order of your ideas.
- Then begin to write your answer.

NOTES

can be something whole family enjoy together   poor diet   TV violence

helps people to sympathize/empathize with others   disappearance of
                                                      family conversation

some people desperate to be famous   informative about national and
                                                      foreign affairs

encourages laziness/non-activity   a 2nd chance at education for some
                                                      people

a lot of non-educational/stupid programmes   cheap source of
                                                      entertainment and
                                                      information

helps people experience countries/culture they can't experience directly

Beneficial effect	Negative effect
informative about national and foreign affairs	

2 Decide which points are similar and can be grouped together.

3 Now decide which you think are the 3 main benefits and 3 most negative points concerning the effect of TV on people's lives. (in your opinion)

4 Look at the three diagrams below. Which is the most appropriate essay structure for a Task 2 answer?

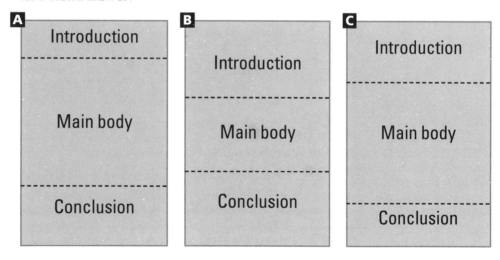

A
Introduction
- - - - - - - -
Main body
- - - - - - - -
Conclusion

B
Introduction
- - - - - - - -
Main body
- - - - - - - -
Conclusion

C
Introduction
- - - - - - - -
Main body
- - - - - - - -
Conclusion

5 Which would be the best overall structure for this question?

Some people believe that television has brought many benefits to people's lives. Others believe that it has had a negative effect. Discuss both of these views and give your own opinions.

A
Para. 1   examples of good programmes
Para. 2   examples of bad programmes
Para. 3   suggestions about future programming

Remember
- A good essay or composition must have a beginning, a middle and an end.
- Decide what you're going to write and make a brief plan outlining what each paragraph will contain.
- Write brief notes on what you want to include in each paragraph. This helps to prompt you as you write your essay and serves as a useful checklist when you have finished.
- A useful guideline to follow is to write an introduction of approximately 50 words, the main body of 170 words or more and a conclusion of 30–40 words. However, these amounts are flexible.

B

Para. 1   a list of the general benefits of TV
Para. 2   specific examples of benefits from personal experience
Para. 3   a list of the general negative effects of TV
Para. 4   specific examples of negative effects from personal experience

C

Para. 1   general comments about the popularity and use of TV
Para. 2   a description of the benefits + examples
Para. 3   a description of the negative effects + examples
Para. 4   a suggestion about how we can benefit the most from TV

The introduction

Aim and contents

- A good introduction includes a general statement about the topic and may provide a guide to the rest of the discussion.
- It may also include the initial views of the writer on this subject – views that will be developed later.
- An introduction must be clear and relevant.

Which introduction below is most suitable for the task about television?

> **Remember**
> - Don't copy out the words in the questions. You will not gain marks for this.
> - The introduction needs to be relevant to the question.
> - Write in an impersonal, formal style.

A
> *Some people believe that television has brought many benefits to people's lives. Others believe that it has had a negative effect. In this essay I will discuss both of these views and give my own opinion about it.*

B
> *There is no doubt that television has transformed people's lives. For many, it has become their prime source of news, entertainment and information. In some affluent societies, a television in every room is not unusual. In poorer countries, a single television may be watched by a large crowd. In both cases, the television can fascinate the viewer.*

C
> *In my house, there's a television in every room. You might think this is unusual but it's because we all like different kinds of programmes. Television can be a good thing if it entertains you. But if there is a big argument about the remote control, everyone just gets annoyed.*

The main body

Aim and contents

- This is the main part of your essay and will develop the key ideas and topic mentioned in the introduction.
- In IELTS Writing Task 2, this section will probably consist of two or three paragraphs.
- This section must be related to the opening and closing paragraphs.

Read the two paragraphs below. There are four main claims (or topic sentences) about the benefits and negative effects of television.

<u>Underline</u> each claim and number them, **1–4**. Highlight the example or supporting sentence that follows.

Clearly, television has become the prime source of information for many people.   1
At the touch of a button, we can find out about the latest economic developments,   2
changes in social policy, political news and so on. **As well as** keeping us in touch   3
with current affairs, television offers us an opportunity to experience countries and 4
cultures that we cannot experience directly. This experience **is** partly **responsible**   5
for the change in British food and our interest in foreign films and music.   6

Despite these benefits, there are certainly a number of problems **associated with** a 7
dependency on television. Firstly, it has been accused of destroying conversation, 8
especially during family meal times. 'How was your day?' has been replaced with 9
'What's on channel three?'. **As** it is such a time-consuming passive activity, it can 10
also lead to health problems. **Whereas** children used to spend a great deal of their 11
free time playing outdoors, they now amuse themselves in front of the TV for 12
hours. This is bad for their general fitness, eyesight and ability to concentrate on 13
more active interests. 14

Linking words and useful phrases

not only does
in particular
it is obvious that   since
related to
there is no doubt that
in comparison to
in addition to   however
has led to   has resulted in
on the other hand
connected to   mainly
because   while

1 Match the words in bold to two other phrases in the box that have a similar meaning.

clearly   ....

as well as   ....

is responsible for   ....

despite   ....

associated with   ....

especially   ....

as   ....

whereas   ....

2 Use the word in brackets to rewrite the sentences below.

(Try to do this exercise from memory. Do not look at the answers to exercise 1.)

a   Clearly, the effects of pollution have become widespread.   (doubt)
b   People often feel under pressure to behave like others in their group. This is especially true for teenagers.   (particular)
c   In the past, most people rarely went abroad whereas now, it is common to take a foreign holiday.   (comparison)
d   The huge amount of fat and sugar in our food is responsible for the modern problem of obesity.   (led)
e   Advertisements encourage people to buy goods they don't need. As well as this, they often make people feel dissatisfied with their lives.   (addition)
f   Despite providing many people with employment, global tourism has often destroyed their environment.   (however)
g   A high crime rate is often associated with high unemployment.   (related)
h   We need to offer free languages courses to recent immigrants and to help them overcome their culture shock.   (not only)
i   The internet and email are responsible for more people working from home. (resulted)

Conclusion

Aim and contents

The concluding paragraph sums up the key points covered in the essay.

Remember
- You can include your own point of view in any conclusion but write in a formal way.
- You should not add new points but you can make a suggestion about what future developments you hope to see.

1 Read the question again and choose the best conclusion for it from **A–C** below. Give your reasons.

Some people believe that television has brought many benefits to people's lives. Others believe that it has had a negative effect. Discuss both of these views and give your own opinions.

A

> In the end, we cannot blame television for people's behaviour. Each person is responsible for deciding how they spend their time. If you find that you are spending more of the day in front of the screen than talking to real people, you know that television has become far too important!

B

> Finally, in my opinion, if you watch too much television, that's your problem. I think you should go out and do other things like normal people.

C

> To sum up, the benefits of television are that it provides information about the news and helps us experience new things. The problems are that it can destroy family conversation and can lead to poor health.

2 Use the words or phrases below to write a different conclusion for this question. There are two possible answers for each gap.

| so that we can   fair to say   ensure   in conclusion   outweigh   to sum up |
| true   outnumber   make sure   in order to |

(a) .... , it is probably (b) .... that the benefits of
television (c) .... its negative effects. What we need to do now is to
(d) .... that television keeps its promise to educate and entertain,
(e) .... improve our lives and not limit them.

Skills practice

Read the task below. Then read the model answer on page 59 and do skills practice exercises 1–4.

In the past people often got married and had children when they were very young. Nowadays many people choose to start a family later on in life.

What do you think are the advantages and disadvantages of this development?

1 Claims and supporting sentences

Find the claims or supporting sentences in each paragraph.

	Claim	Supporting sentence or example
Introduction *example*	*more people having children in their thirties/forties*	*not necessary – the claim is made in the task*
Paragraph 2	*Older people more financially secure* ————————— —————————	————————— ————————— *Parents lose sleep/must give up a lot of their free time*
Paragraph 3	————————— *big generation gap* —————————	*Parents tired when children want to play* ————————— *Little interaction/little support*
Conclusion	*Impossible to generalize about best time to have children*	————————— —————————

It is certainly true that until recently most couples got married and had children in 1
their early or mid twenties sometimes even earlier. However, there is now a 2
definite trend towards having children in your thirties even early forties. How will 3
this development effect the family 4

One reason for starting a family later is that the parents are usually more financially
secure than younger couples this means that they can provide a decent house and 5
have a regular job or savings to support their children. Furthermore new parents 6
will lose a lot of sleep and will have to give up much of their free time to look after
their baby's needs. Raising young children therefore requires patience and 7
flexibility. Older couples may have acquired these skills through their
greater life experience.

Having said that taking care of a child is a physically-demanding task. It may be 8
the case that older parents become tired when their child still wants to play. As well
as this the greater generation gap may mean that parents and their teenagers have 9
little in common. For this reason they may find it difficult to communicate and 10
understand each other's way of thinking. Unfortunately it is also true that the 11
children's grandparents may be elderly and unable to have much interaction with
them. Nowadays it is common to hear parents complain that they have no support 12
from family.

In conclusion we cannot really generalize about the best time to have a child. It 13
depends on the personality and personal circumstances of each potential mother or
father. The most important thing is simply that the child is loved and looked after.

2 Linking words

Read the essay above again. Find linking words or phrases for each category below.

Addition	Contrast	Cause	Consequence
1	1	1	1
2			2

3 Useful words and phrases

Find a phrase which is used to ...

a make a definite claim

b introduce an advantage

c make a possible claim

d Find a verb that means 'to make a general statement about something'.

4 Punctuation

Read the essay again. You need to add 12 commas (,) 1 semi-colon (;) and
1 question mark. (?) Add the punctuation to the numbered lines only.

TASK RESPONSE	Has the student understood the task question? Do the contents of the essay provide a suitable and full response?
COHERENCE AND COHESION	Is the essay well organized? Can you follow the student's argument without difficulty? Is there a logical connection between clauses, sentences or ideas?
LEXICAL RESOURCE	Is there a good range of vocabulary in the essay? Is the vocabulary formal enough for this type of essay?
GRAMMATICAL RANGE AND ACCURACY	Is there a good range of grammatical structures? Is the grammar generally correct or are there many mistakes that make the essay difficult to understand?

Read the question below again. Do you remember what the main topic and task are?

People who live and work in large cities often complain that they are suffering from stress. What do you think are the causes of this problem and how should it be solved?

Read the students' answers below and make notes.

Sample answer 1:

In this world, there are big cities and this cities has problem. Also the people who live there they feel difficulty to keep on life buecause the stress.

On the one hand, the crowds in cities is a problem. All people they want to drive around the cities and it is very difficult for the car of police or ambulance to move quickly in cities if they has emergency call because that I think the government should get tax for drivers who want to parking his cars in the city centre for more then half an hour. Also in the morning all people go to work and student to schools the cities become busy for that the government should give more public transport to be easy for people to travel.

In addition, noisy is the biggest and the most important problem in any cities. The head of noisy is come from the horn motorbikes and gas engines. Because that the government ought to install more traffic light in one road. Also, the government should charge for who have car to impose people to change to taxi, bus or train and it is very helpful to have less crowds in cities such as London. The people in London ues taxi, bus or underground to move or to go to work and London is the lessest cities crowd or noisy in the world.

In my opinion I agree the people who live or work in big cities feel stress. Also I think in the future the government will have solved for this problem.

Marwan Salem Saeed Al Khatri

---

285 words

TASK RESPONSE	COHERENCE AND COHESION	LEXICAL RESOURCE	GRAMMATICAL RANGE AND ACCURACY

Sample answer 2:

Nowadays, more and more big cities are appeared in the world. Undoubtedly, that is an advantage for the economy development. But there are also some drawbacks. For example, people who live and work in large cities are suffering from different kinds of stress.

Usually, the population in the large city is very high. People tend to use their private cars to go wherever they like, so it causes a serious traffic problem. Most people don't have the patient to wait in a traffic jam. Maybe they will lose their job if they cannot arrive at their destination on time.

Most of the people love quiet, they don't like to stay in a crowded environment if it is unnecessary. That will make them feel nervous. If you are living in a large city and you want to relax, but there are too many people on the street, that make you cannot do what you want and you cannot go to the places that you want. It will make you feel sad. That makes the stress staying in your mind.

There are some ways to solve those problems. Firstly, about the traffic problem, some green organisation can persuade the people to use more public transport and the government can increase road tax. That can make the people use public transport, so the traffic can be reduced and not be so busy. Secondly, the government can transfer some businesses and industries outside the city. That can reduce the population in some of the popular places.

People are suffering different kinds of stress nowadays. If the government can do more about this, this problem must be solved quickly in the future.

Amy

277 words

TASK ACHIEVEMENT	COHERENCE AND COHESION	LEXICAL RESOURCE	GRAMMATICAL RANGE AND ACCURACY

Language work

1 Read Amy's essay again. Most of the errors have been corrected and some sentences have been replaced to improve it.

Choose the correct linking word or phrase from the box on page 62 to complete the essay.

Nowadays, more and more big cities are appearing in the world. Undoubtedly, that is an advantage for a country's economic development. (1) ...., there are also some drawbacks, for example, people who live and work there often suffer from different kinds of stress.

Usually, the population in a large city is very high. People tend to use their private cars to go wherever they like, (2) .... this causes a serious traffic problem. Most people don't have the patience to wait in a traffic jam. (3) ...., they often worry that perhaps they will lose their job if they cannot arrive at their destination on time.

Most people love peace and quiet (4) .... they don't like to stay in a crowded environment (5) .... this will make them feel nervous. If you are living in a large city and you want to relax, (6) .... there are too many people on the street, that means you cannot do what you want and you cannot go to the places that you would like. (7) .... kind of situation makes you feel sad and stressed.

(8) .... problems could be solved in the following ways. Firstly, (9) .... the traffic problem, some green organisations could persuade people to use more public transport and the government could increase road tax. (10) .... would reduce the amount of traffic on the road. Secondly, the government could transfer some businesses and industries outside the city (11) .... would reduce the population in some of the more populated places.

People are suffering different kinds of stress nowadays. If the government decided to do more about this, this problem would soon be solved.

this	regarding	so	moreover	which	because
but	these	and for this reason		however	this

2 True or False?

a   *Regarding* can be replaced with *Concerning*   T/F

b   *Moreover* can be replaced by *Furthermore*   T/F

c   *which* can always be replaced by *that*   T/F

d   *however* and *but* can have the same meaning   T/F

e   we can put *so* at the beginning of a sentence to show a result   T/F

Further practice

You should spend about 40 minutes on this task.

Write about the following topic:

In Britain, many traditions and customs are changing or have disappeared completely.

What is the situation in your country?

Give reasons for your answer and include any relevant examples from your own knowledge or experience.

Write at least 250 words.

Study Skills: Speaking

How much do you know about the IELTS Speaking module?

Do the quiz below to find out.

Quiz

1 How long is the Speaking module?
  A 15–20 minutes
  B 11–14 minutes
  C 40–45 minutes

2 There are three main parts of the Speaking module. Are these statements about the three Parts true or false?

Part 1

1 This Part lasts between four and five minutes.
2 The candidate is asked to describe a picture.
3 The candidate answers general questions about themselves, their families, their jobs and other familiar topics.

Part 2

4 The candidate is given a minute to prepare to talk about a topic.
5 The candidate is asked to talk about a topic for ten minutes.
6 The candidate must choose what topic they wish to discuss.

Part 3

7 This Part lasts between four and five minutes.
8 This Part is a discussion between the candidate and examiner on a topic related to Part 2.
9 This is the easiest Part of the module.

Part 1

Talking about familiar topics

In Part 1 of the Speaking module, you have to answer questions about familiar topics. You can't know exactly what you will be asked, but you can prepare.

Look at the topics below. Write questions that the examiner might ask you about them. Then look at the suggestions on page 98.
  • Your studies
  • Your previous work experience, your current job or your future career plans
  • Your family/home life
  • Your country
  • Your hobbies and interests

Giving a good answer

1 Read some possible questions and answers for Part 1. Tick the answers that you think are good.

A **Examiner:** Who was your favourite teacher at school? Why did you like their lessons?
Candidate: Mr Wallis. Because they were easy.

B **Examiner:** How long have you been studying English?
Candidate: I am very interested in English because it is a world language and I hope it will help me to do well in my career.

C **Examiner:** What do you do?
Candidate: Well, at the moment I'm studying full time, but back in my country I'm a doctor and I hope to be able to find work here as a doctor too.

D **Examiner:** What are the best things about your job?
Candidate: Oh, definitely the people. I love meeting people from all over the world.

E **Examiner:** Do you live with your family?
Candidate: No.

F **Examiner:** How long have you been in the UK?
Candidate: I will stay three years.

G **Examiner:** Tell me about where you are living at the moment.
Candidate: It is a, er, er, what is the word, er, er, maisonette!

H **Examiner:** Do you enjoy travelling?
Candidate: Yes, I'm really interested in seeing the world. While I've been living in Britain, I've also taken the opportunity to go to Europe and see France and Spain. I found the people in Spain really friendly.

2 How can you improve the other answers?

3 Now record yourself answering the same questions. Listen to the recording and evaluate your performance.

Useful language

At the moment I'm living/studying/working …
Before that I lived in …
Recently, I've been to France/started playing football, etc.
(*note the use of the present perfect here*)
I'm planning to …
After that I'll probably …

I prefer (*followed by a noun*) Scotland because …
I'd rather (*followed by verb*) live in Australia because …

Both my father and mother …
Neither of my brothers …
None of my friends …

It depends. Sometimes I like cooking, and sometimes I'm just too tired.
Definitely, I love it! It's …
Mmm, possibly. It depends on the weather really.
Generally I think it's a good idea because …
Well, it's very different because …

Let me think/see, …
I'm not really sure, but perhaps …
That's a good question/point. I suppose …
I haven't really given that much thought before but …

---

4 Write answers that are true for you to the questions below.

1 Why are you taking IELTS?
2 What are your ambitions?
3 Tell me about where you are living at the moment.
4 How would you describe your home town?
5 What do you usually do at the weekend?

Identifying strengths and weaknesses

Remember
- Make sure you answer the question.
- One-word answers are not acceptable.
- Always add some extra information to your answer.

1 🔲 23 Listen to a student answering the examiner's questions. What is good about their performance? How could it be improved? Use the checklist to help you and refer to the Recording script on page 108.

Checklist
- Does the student answer the questions correctly?
- Does she answer the questions fully, giving extra information?
- Is her grammar accurate?
- Does she use a range of vocabulary appropriately?
- Is it easy to understand her pronunciation?
- Does she use any words or phrases to make her language sound more natural, eg *Well, Actually, Oh definitely*, etc.?
- Does she sound fluent or does she often hesitate?

---

2 Now record yourself answering the same questions (see page 108 for the questions). Listen to the recording and evaluate your performance using the checklist above.

Planning your answer

In Part 2 of the Speaking module you have to speak for 1–2 minutes on a topic. You have one minute to think about this topic. Use this time well.

1 Read the sample question below. <u>Underline</u> the key words in the instructions.

> Describe an occasion when you have been successful. You should say:
> • where and when you were successful
> • how you were successful
> • what you had to do to make sure you were successful
> and describe how you felt about your success.

2 Think of two or three things to say about each part of the question. You can make notes if you wish, but remember you only have **one** minute.

Giving extra information

It is important that you talk for long enough: minimum one minute and maximum two minutes. This means you have to think of extra information to give the examiner. You can do this in different ways by:
• saying why you think/feel something
• giving examples
• giving details

1 Read this sample question and <u>underline</u> the key words.

> Talk about an important day in your life. You should say:
> • when this day was
> • if you were alone or with others
> • where you were and what happened
> and explain why this day was important to you.

2 Think of relevant things to say about each part of the question. Give examples and include details.

3 Use the different parts of the question to organize your answer, so that each part follows on logically from the one before.

4 🎙️ 24 Now listen to this student answering the question. Does he include all of the main points?

Remember
It is important to keep talking, but don't talk about things which are not related to the topic.

Useful language

The best/worst thing about ... is/was ...
The thing I really like(d)/hate(d) about ... is/was ...
One of the problems with ... is/was ...

I particularly remember ... because ...
I'll never forget ... because ...

5 Look at the *Useful language* box and practise answering the two sample questions. Time yourself to check your answers are the right length.

Describe a present someone gave you which was/is important to you.
You should say:
- what the present was
- who gave it to you
- why they gave it to you (eg to celebrate a birthday)
and explain why it is so important to you.

Describe a friend who has played an important part in your life. You should say:
- how you met this person
- how long you have known them
- the kind of things you do or did with them
and explain why they have been important in your life.

Identifying strengths and weaknesses

25 Listen to answers to the second sample question. Which one is a better answer? Why?

Follow-up questions

After you have spoken for 1–2 minutes, the examiner may ask you one or two follow-up questions about what you have said. For example:

Question	Answer	Follow-up question
How did you feel when you arrived in the UK?	I was very nervous because I didn't know anybody.	Did you find it easy to meet people?

1 Match the appropriate answers **A–F** to questions **1–6**.

1 Do you enjoy playing sports?
2 Would you like to go there again?
3 Do you think it will be easy to get a job in IT?
4 Have you ever been to any other countries in Europe?
5 Would you consider doing the same sort of job again?
6 Would you recommend the holiday to other people?

A No, not really. It wasn't very good value for money.
B I don't think so. It wasn't really for me.
C I expect so. It's a growing industry.
D Yes, definitely. I particularly enjoy outdoor ones.
E Possibly. It would depend on who I went with!
F Yes, a few. France, Spain and the Czech Republic.

2 26 Listen and check.

3 26 Listen again and repeat the answers.

Part 3

Remember
- One-word answers are **not** acceptable.
- Always give a reason for your answer.

Expanding answers

In Part 3 of the Speaking module, you have to discuss questions related to the topic in Part 2 with the examiner. Although this is a discussion, you should do most of the talking. Sometimes the examiner will ask you questions which seem to need a one word answer. For example:

1 Is it a good idea to exercise regularly?
2 Is there more crime these days?
3 Do you think everyone should have a mobile phone?

1 Read the example questions above again. Write an answer for each including a reason.

2 Now add an extra sentence or two to each of your answers.

Linking ideas

1 The words and phrases in the box are all used to link ideas. Put them into the appropriate categories below.

| on the other hand   and   so   because   however   such as |

1 the reason for something
2 the result of something
3 joining two ideas together
4 contrasting two ideas
5 giving an example

2 Look at the *Useful language* boxes and practise giving answers to questions 1–8 below.

Useful language: Comparing and contrasting

On the one hand … on the other hand …
Well, … isn't as … as …
… is nowhere near as … as …

I'd rather …
I'd much prefer (to) …

It depends (on) …

Useful language: Making predictions/talking about the future

There's a good chance that …
I doubt very much if …

I hope that …
I expect that …
I'm afraid that … (*this does not mean you feel fear, but is a way of talking about something negative, eg I'm afraid that a lot of smokers will complain, but …*)
It's bound to (+ *infinitive*)

It is/isn't very likely to …

Useful language: Giving opinions

As far as I'm concerned …
It seems to me that …
I can't help thinking that … (*use this phrase when you think that people won't agree with you*)
I tend to think that …
I strongly believe that …

1 Do you think smoking will be banned in all public places?
2 Do you prefer to go out or stay at home in the evening?
3 Do you think that email has made our lives easier?
4 Which is better: living in the countryside or in the city?
5 Are qualifications important?
6 How likely is it that computers will be able to do your job in future?
7 Would you rather watch sport or play it?
8 What do you think the consequences of global warming will be?

3 27 Now listen to students answering the eight questions above.
- Do they give full answers?
- Do they use a range of vocabulary?
- Are their answers grammatically correct?

Practice test

Section 1   Questions 1–10

Questions 1 and 2

Circle the appropriate letter.

1 Where does the man study?
   A Aston University
   B William's University
   C Birmingham University
   D Edgbaston University

2 What kind of property does the man want?
   A a three bedroom flat
   B a two bedroom property
   C a one bedroom house with a garden
   D a property with a garage

Questions 3–6

Complete the table. Write **NO MORE THAN THREE WORDS OR A NUMBER** for each answer.

	Flat 1	Flat 2
Location	Edgbaston	(3) ....
Floor	ground floor	(4) ....
Furnished?	(5)	fully furnished
Price	£480 pcm	(6) .... pcm

Question 7

Circle the appropriate letter.

7 Which of the following are included in the rent?

A gas
B water rates
C electricity
D phone

Questions 8–10

Complete the notes.

Property address:
(8) ....
Name of client: *John Taylor*
Contact phone number:
(9) *0791* ....
Meet at: (10) .... *p.m.*

Section 2   Questions 11–20

Questions 11–15

Complete the summary. Write **NO MORE THAN THREE WORDS** for each answer.

> ### Dangers at the beach in Sydney
>
> Shark attacks are not very common, about **(11)** ....
> take place each year, and box jellyfish are only a problem further
> **(12)** .... Another danger at the beach is
> **(13)** ...., and you should slip on a shirt, slap on a
> **(14)** .... and slop on some sun cream. Far less
> **(15)** .... are rip currents which you are more likely
> to die from than anything else.

Questions 16–18

Complete the labels on the diagram. Write **NO MORE THAN THREE WORDS** for each answer.

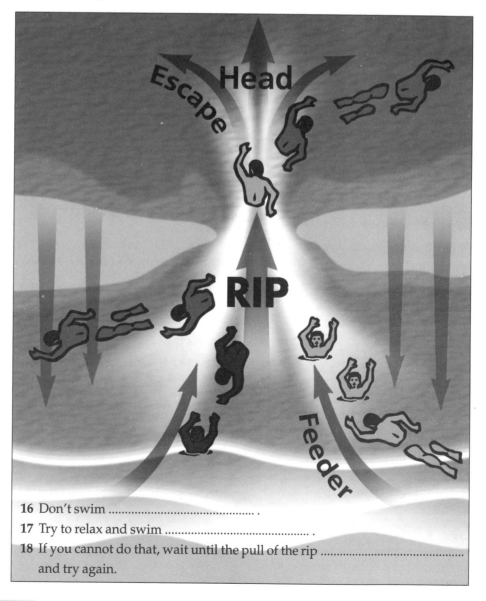

16 Don't swim ....

17 Try to relax and swim ....

18 If you cannot do that, wait until the pull of the rip ....
and try again.

Questions 19 and 20

Complete the sentences. Write **NO MORE THAN THREE WORDS** for each answer.

19 To be safe in the ocean, don't ....

20 Only swim in places where you can see ....

Section 3   Questions 21–30

Questions 21–24

Answer the questions. Write **NO MORE THAN THREE WORDS** for each answer.

21 What subject is Andrew studying?
22 Name the crop that Andrew mentions.
23 Which disadvantage of using chemicals does Andrew mention?
24 Why might insects be beneficial to the farmer?

Questions 25–27

Circle **THREE** appropriate letters **A–F**.

Insects which are beneficial to crop plants are:

A butterflies
B snails
C beetles
D wasps
E caterpillars
F slugs

Questions 28–30

Complete the summary. Write **NO MORE THAN THREE WORDS** for each answer.

A ring of insecticide is **(28)** .... around the tree trunk,

and then the tree is sprayed with a chemical called *pyrethrum*, made from

(29) .... The insects drop from the tree, and only the

ones with **(30)** .... are able to return safely.

Section 4   Questions 31–40

Questions 31–35

Complete the sentences. Write **NO MORE THAN THREE WORDS OR A NUMBER** for each answer.

31 Two kinds of ownership are mentioned: a sole proprietorship and a

....

32 A corporation has the same legal rights as a ....

33 A board can be as small as ....

34 Shareholders meet .... to vote for the people on the board.

35 The board is like the human brain because they ....

Questions 36–39

Complete the flow chart. Write **NO MORE THAN THREE WORDS OR A NUMBER** for each answer.

How a corporation works

A business idea is generated

⬇

(36) .... is needed

⬇

A corporation is formed

⬇

(37) .... are sold to raise revenue

⬇

Money is invested in equipment and (38) ....

⬇

Company makes (39) ....

⬇

Dividend paid to shareholders

Question 40

Circle the appropriate letter.

40 Another advantage of a corporation is that
    A you can't go out of business.
    B you can't lose everything you own.
    C you can get sued.
    D you and the restaurant are legally the same.

Reading

Section 1

Questions 1–8

Look at the extract from a guide book on Ireland on page 72.

Complete the sentences below with words taken from the passage.

Write **NO MORE THAN THREE WORDS** for each answer.

1 In July and August it is difficult to get ....
2 .... are often closed during winter months.
3 Most special events happen in ....
4 .... may be unavailable for some visitor attractions.
5 Drivers without a European Union licence may drive for

....
6 For most tourist attractions, it is possible to join a ....
7 You should stay in a .... to meet people.
8 You'll be able to .... at most hostels.

TRAVELLING IN IRELAND: FACTS FOR THE VISITOR

When to go

The weather is generally warm in July and August and the daylight hours are long, but the crowds are greater, the costs higher and accommodation is hard to find. If you go in winter there are fewer tourists and accommodation is cheaper, but you may get miserable weather, the daylight hours are short and many tourist facilities are shut. It's worth considering visiting Ireland in September, when the weather can be better than in the winter, it's less crowded than in the summer, and most attractions and tourist offices are open. Festivals and other events occur throughout the year, with July and August being the busiest months.

What kind of trip?

Your particular interests will have a large influence on the kind of trip you choose, as will the amount of time and money you have. Try to leave enough time for a cycle ride along one or two countryside trails and you won't be disappointed. Some visitor attractions have no public transport so walking or cycling may be your only way to see them. You may also want to consider hiring a car to visit some remote places. Unless you have a European Union driving licence, your licence is valid up to 12 months from the date of entry into Ireland. However, the majority of attractions can be visited as part of a guided tour. Travelling alone is a great way to get to know fellow travelers and campsites are great places for sharing stories and experiences.

What to bring

A raincoat or an umbrella is a necessity, as are some warm clothes – even during warm summer weather it gets chilly in the evenings. A sleeping bag is useful in hostels and for campsites. A sheet is necessary if you plan to stay in hostels, though they usually lend them out for a small charge if you don't bring your own.

Questions 9–14

Look at the six job advertisements **A–F** on page 73.

For which job are the following statements true?

Write the correct letter **A–F**.

Example	
It may be necessary to make your own decisions at times.	**D**

9   It is necessary to travel to different places as part of your daily routine.
10 It is part of the job to tell other staff what they need to do.
11 There may be times when you have to work at weekends.
12 It is not necessary to have worked in this kind of position before.
13 There may be a chance to get a better position in the company.
14 It is possible to choose when you want to work.

A

HARDING-HARRIS CONSTRUCTION
CARPENTERS WANTED
IN LONDON

There are many reasons why you should apply to us:

- We have excellent relationships with staff, clients, and suppliers.
- We are one of England's busiest construction companies with branches in Manchester, London and Portsmouth.
- We employ over 250 staff.
- We offer medical insurance after 3 months.

Please apply to ...

B

KINDERCARE
Home Teachers

We seek enthusiastic people to join our Kindercare service. Your responsibilities include visiting children in their own home and assisting with their learning and development. There are several positions of 35 hours per week. Teachers usually make three to four visits per day. Applicants should have a Diploma of Teaching.

Please send your CV to ...

C

Retail Opportunities

We have exciting opportunities available for sales people in our Lewisham store. If you:

- enjoy working in a team environment
- have at least two years retail experience
- wish to join a company that offers real opportunities to advance into senior and management roles

then we want to hear from you.
Please write to ...

D

CITY STADIUM
PART TIME
OFFICE ADMINISTRATOR

We need an efficient person with good communication skills and excellent knowledge of Microsoft Excel to be responsible for office administration. During busy periods, you will be need to think for yourself and work unsupervised. The position is part time during the day. We can be flexible with days and hours of work to fit in with your schedule.

Please contact ...

E

DENTAL RECEPTIONIST

We require a dental receptionist for our busy dental practice in Lee Green, S.E.London. Must have: professional attitude, excellent communication skills, be motivated, hard working and want to be part of a team. No experience necessary as full training will be given.
Please send your CV to ...

F

FITNESS INSTRUCTOR

You will provide fitness advice to people of all ages and promote a safe and fun environment. You must have the ability to lead a team and will be the senior fitness instructor on duty. You will have a Diploma in Fitness Training and a current First Aid Certificate. Some hours will be on Saturdays, Sundays and one evening per week.

If you are interested please write to ...

CERTIFICATE IN CARPENTRY

The certificate in carpentry (level three) offers entry into a career in building and construction. Aimed at school-leavers and mature students looking to retrain, this one-year pre-trade full time course gives students the skills needed for a wide variety of carpentry-related jobs. Fully equipped workshops and staff with industry experience enable students to complete qualifications at many levels, says Kerry Brown, senior lecturer at the institute.

Students who complete the 120 credits needed for the certificate in carpentry can progress to the (60 credits) one-semester (18-week) certificate in carpentry (level four).

Subjects taught during the 36-week certificate in carpentry (level three) programme include: identifying and selecting materials from drawings; setting out and supervising the placements of foundations; and fixing internal floors, walls, and ceiling linings.

Students enrolling for the certificate need to have completed three years of secondary education or fill one of the following criteria: be employed in the industry; have a work history confirmed by references; or have company sponsorship that may lead to employment once they've finished the course.

Applicants must also be fluent in spoken and written English language and be physically able to complete the practical aspects of the programme.

Classes are held three days a week, Monday, Tuesday and Wednesday or Wednesday, Thursday and Friday from 8am to 4.30pm. Students are encouraged to seek or continue employment while they're studying and the institute can help to find work.

Opportunities available to graduates, says Brown, range from employment within the building industry as a carpenter, specialist craftsperson, building supervisor, or project manager, through to self-employed builder or property developer.

While there are no formal examinations at the end of the level 3 certificate course, students are assessed in the practical and theoretical aspects of what they have learnt. They can also decide to sit exams for theory components of the National Certificate in Carpentry.

The programme, which costs around $4467, has up to 32 places per course. Students can apply for next year's February and July level three intakes right up until each course begins.

Questions 15–21

Do the following statements agree with the information given in the course description on page 74?

Write

TRUE if the statement agrees with the information
FALSE if the statement contradicts the information
NOT GIVEN if there is no information on this

15 The carpentry course is specially designed for people who just left school.
16 Most students who take the level 3 course go on to take the level 4 course.
17 Applicants must have attended secondary school for 3 years or be working in the industry.
18 It is necessary for students to have passed an English language examination.
19 The institute thinks students should work during the course.
20 Students can choose whether or not to take an examination in carpentry.
21 The carpentry course runs twice a year.

STUDY AT WF EDUCATION LANGUAGE AND TRAVEL

SWANSEA, WALES

WF Education Language and Travel are a small, independent organisation but with an excellent reputation for the quality, value and standard of our English instruction. We pride ourselves on offering a friendly service which is one reason why so many of our clients return. We specialise in running short intensive courses in General and Business English for individuals or small groups.

Our group courses are for clients from the same organisation. We do not hold mixed nationality courses, nor do we run courses for youngsters. Our normal minimum age is 25 years, but most of our clients hold senior executive positions within their organisations; so clients in their 40s and 50s form a major part of our business. Group courses will be for 2 to 10 participants.

An individual course is intensive and demanding because you speak and hear English all the time and have no opportunity to use your mother tongue. It is, however, the *fast track* method to improve your English. Such concentration, although challenging, will ensure maximum progress in the minimum time. Two week courses are always available but longer periods of study can also be arranged. Courses are held throughout the year and, because each is structured to meet your learning and business requirements, you can choose to start and finish your course on any day of the week whenever you like.

We offer a unique arrangement – you stay with a host family and your lessons are held in the family home. You are taught by two experienced teachers each with special areas of expertise. Our package includes 5 hours of English a day but if you feel this would be too much you can choose to study for only 3 or 4 hours per day.

You will use material we think best suited to your needs based on a test we ask you to complete before your arrival in Swansea and an assessment we make at the beginning of your course. We are happy for you to bring work with you so that, for example, if you have to present a paper in English or write a report – we will help you with the preparation.

Questions 22–27

Complete the summary of information below.

Choose **NO MORE THAN THREE WORDS** or a **NUMBER** from the text on page 75 for each answer.

WF Education Language and Travel can offer English language classes which are of a high quality, value and standard. Individuals as well as small groups can take **(example)** *(short intensive) courses* .... either in General or Business English. For organisations who wish to book a group course, they should be aware that the students need to be of the same **(22)** .... and at least 25 years old. However, clients on group courses usually tend to be older and be working at management level. The minimum class size is two. For students who wish to make the most **(23)** .... but do not have much time, it is recommended that they take an individual course. Although these usually run for a **(24)** .... period, students can ask to extend their studies. It is also possible to book the exact course dates you want. Unlike most other schools, lessons for individuals are held in the house where they live and students will benefit from the **(25)** .... of two, experienced teachers. Lessons usually last **(26)** .... although a student can decide to reduce this. Students are required to take a test to show their English ability, and this together with the **(27)** .... carried out at the start of the course will help the school design a course to meet individual needs.

The inhumane race

Modern living seems designed to doing everything at an increasingly fast rate. Is there a way to challenge the cult of speed?

A

At my local supermarket, it takes an average of 23 seconds to process my credit card payment. Resisting an urge to drum my fingers on the counter, I stare at the screen, willing it to show that my card is 'Accepted'. The checkout operator whose shift is punctuated by these delays, gazes into space, having already followed her 'customer engagement' instruction with a flash of eye contact and a quick "How's your day been so far?" To this question, my answer is always the same: "Busy".

B

And we are. A staggering 94 percent of managers said they regularly received work-related calls out of hours, time that they should be relaxing and spending with their family. And these days even

micro-delays try our patience. The elderly driver going at 5kph less than the speed limit, the slow-loading web page, the ATM 'fast cash' that takes its own sweet time to cough up. Switch on the TV and you'll see there are now faster toasters, express irons that heat up more quickly, instant digital photos, speed dial, answering machines that play back 25 percent faster. The Sony Discman allows users to close the gaps of CDs "so you can enjoy playing with less blank space between tracks". But nothing satisfies our need for speed.

C

In 1959, cardiologists Meyer Friedman and Ray Rosenman used the term 'Type A' personality to describe the pathologically impatient male who is driving himself to a heart attack. "How can I move faster, and do more and more things in less and less time?" is the question that never ceases to torment him." Today, Type A behaviour is common, applicable not only to male executives, but also to teachers, clerks, factory workers, part-time working mothers and even children.

D

In what has been called the 'Everydayathon' of modern life, time seems to have contracted. Dr Larry Dossey, who coined the term 'hurry sickness', used to ask his patients to sit quietly in a chair and say when they think a minute had elapsed. The record went to a manager who said "That's a minute" after only nine seconds. Dossey believes that this common distortion of time is more than an example of psychologically odd behaviour. "The perceptions of passing time that we observe from our external clocks cause our internal clocks to run faster." In the long term, that may lead to heart disease or high blood pressure.

E

Managers make sympathetic noises when employees express their anxiety about their workload, but stop short of suggesting that they work less. If anything, the trend is to 'overtasking', the constant upward resetting of goals and targets. More often than not, it proves counter-productive. In the 90s, the new business word was 're-engineering': organisations doing more with less. Employees were manipulated into working even harder by creating competing teams within organisations and using peer pressure within the group to extract extra performance from even the most reluctant. Employees who would have refused to meet unrealistic targets to make the boss look good felt compelled to overwork to avoid letting down their teammates.

F

At the same time, technology accelerated the pace of the working day. Email created the expectation of an instant response to orders, queries and requests, and mobile phones always meant employees were on an electronic leash, 365 days a year. Businesses are now starting to use texting because the abbreviated messages save time and money and cut out idle chat on the phone. To cope with the daily rush, employees have had to make themselves more machine-like by multi-tasking, a term first used for computers in the 1960s.

G

What made it harder for overworked employees was that they knew the rules had changed. The unwritten social contract that if you worked hard, the

organisation would see you right had proved to be an illusion. In the global marketplace, trust, loyalty and commitment had turned out to be a pretence: your fate was just as likely to be determined by anonymous shareholders in Tokyo or Wisconsin. Nor was there extra compensation for that new job insecurity. As the gap between executive and workers' salaries continued to grow, ordinary employees were just given non-cash recognition: picnics, gift vouchers and the like, and their salaries remained stagnant.

H

It didn't matter, though, how disgruntled employees were becoming. As Joanna B Cuilla says in her book *The Working Life*, "Organisations no longer need to rely on people having a moral commitment to work. Shopping malls, debt and the advertising industry turn everybody, even moody teenagers, into obedient workers and customers." Many studies have shown that work also shapes our leisure time. "When work is dull, tiresome or stressful, people are sometimes unable to do anything satisfying in their leisure," says Cuilla. "The more time demands of work dominate our lives, the more all activities seem like work. The clock and the schedule rob our social life of spontaneity. It is becoming rare to drop into a friend's house unannounced as we assume our friends are busy at home and don't want to be disturbed."

I

In an article on why smart people underperform, psychiatrist Edward M Hallowell warned that modern office life was turning many people into stressed-out underachievers. Hallowell has coined the term Attention Deficit Trait (ADT) for a condition that he says is now endemic. "The core symptoms are distractibility, inner chaos and impatience. People with ADT have difficulty staying organised, setting priorities and managing time. Indeed, modern culture almost requires many of us to develop ADT. Never in history has the human brain been asked to track so many data points." When the brain is asked to do too much, it shifts us into survival mode, says Hallowell. The result is that the brain simply reverts back to simple black and white thinking. "Intelligence dims. In a futile attempt to do more than is possible, the brain paradoxically reduces the ability to think clearly."

Glossary
contracted (to contract = to grow smaller)
counter-productive = acting against efficiency
multi-tasking = performing a number of tasks at the same time

Section 3

Questions 28–40

Multiple choice

28 What does the writer find particularly annoying at the supermarket checkout?
    A the time he has to wait for his payment to be accepted.
    B the rude attitude of the person who is serving him.
    C the time that it takes for him to move forward in the queue.
    D the unnecessary question that the checkout operator asks him.

29 What does Dr Larry Dossey say about the observation of passing time?
    A Managers tend to think time has passed more quickly than it has.
    B The inability to judge time accurately is often a result of illness.
    C Looking at clocks makes people think time is passing quickly.
    D People are unlikely to make an accurate observation under test conditions.

30 According to the writer, why did employees in the 1990s feel obliged to work harder?
    A They knew they were competing with other companies.
    B Other workers in their company were putting pressure on them.
    C They wanted their managers to notice their performance.
    D Many companies had suffered a decrease in profits.

31 Which of the following best summarizes the writer's argument in paragraph E?
    A Companies offered job security to employees who demonstrated loyalty.
    B Employees needed to look at their employment contracts more carefully.
    C Companies realized they had to offer rewards to keep junior workers happy.
    D Employees realized that there was no point in them working hard.

32 What point is made by the references to Attention Deficit Trait?
    A The modern lifestyle has stopped people working efficiently.
    B Only a certain type of person is able to concentrate on many tasks.
    C The human brain needs to evolve to cope with today's demands.
    D People should set priorities and concentrate on one thing at a time.

Questions 33–39

The passage on pages 76–77 has nine paragraphs labelled **A–I**.

Which paragraph contains the following information?

Write the correct letter **A–I**.

You may use any letter more than once.

33 a description of the way managers deal with complaints about stress

34 examples of how work pressure affects relationships

35 reasons why technology has made life harder for employees

36 an example of how people are still obliged to work during their free time

37 the fact that most kinds of people now want to do things faster

38 reasons why unhappy employees continue to work

39 an example of how the advantage of speed is promoted to consumers

40 What is the overall purpose of this article?
    A to criticize people's over-dependence on technology
    B to highlight the importance of reducing stress
    C to discuss the responsibilities of managers
    D to describe how people have grown more impatient

Task 1

You should spend about twenty minutes on this task.

You recently lost something that is important to you. You want to try to get it back by asking people for help.

Write a letter to the local newspaper. In the letter

- *describe the object that you lost*
- *say where you think you lost it*
- *say why it is important to you*

Write at least 150 words.

You do **NOT** need to write any addresses.

Begin your letter as follows:

To the editor,

Task 2

You should spend about 40 minutes on this task.

Write about the following topic:

Poverty is a problem that affects many people in many countries. Some people believe that it is the government's responsibility to help them. Others believe that poor people should do more to help themselves.

Discuss both these views and give your own opinion.

Give reasons for your answer and include any relevant examples from your own knowledge or experience.

Write at least 250 words.

Part 1

The examiner asks you some general questions about yourself, your home, your job or your studies. For example:

- Do you enjoy living here?
- What are the best things about your country?
- Tell me about your family.
- What are your hobbies?

Part 2

The examiner gives you a card with questions similar to those below. You have one minute to think about the topic and make notes if you wish. You should then talk about the topic for 1–2 minutes.

> Describe a happy event in your childhood that you remember well. You should say:
> - when the event took place
> - where the event took place
> - what happened exactly
> and explain why you remember this event clearly.

When you have finished the examiner, asks a few brief questions about what you have said. For example:
- Did you ever do this again?
- What did your parents think about it?

Part 3

The examiner will ask some discussion questions related to the same topic. For example:

- Do you think children's lives are very different nowadays?
- Are children too protected now?
- Do you think children can have too many toys?
- Is it important to celebrate birthdays and other festivals?

Answer key

Quiz p. 7

1 **B** The Listening module is about 40 minutes long – 30 minutes of listening and 10 minutes at the end to transfer your answers to the answer sheet.
2 **A** There are four Sections.
3 **C** There are 40 questions which may include multiple choice, short answers, filling in charts/diagrams/tables, sentence completion, matching and classifying.
4 True. The texts and questions get more difficult with each Section.
5 True. All the sections are worth the same number of marks, even though the exam gets more difficult.
6 Adam … **C**   1C
  Professor Jones … **A**   2B
  Steve, Mary and Sarah … **D**   3D
  Mr Green … **B**   4A
7 ONCE.
8 Yes. Before each Section, you have about 30 seconds to read the questions for that section.
9 On the question paper, and then transfer them at the end to the answer sheet.
10 True.

Prediction p. 7

1 From the questions, you can predict that a girl, who is probably new to a place, is asking directions from someone. You'll need to listen for a time such as *a week ago* for question 1. As there are several doors to choose from in question 3, she could be looking for an office or a classroom.

2 1 **A**: 'I only arrived here yesterday'
  2 **C**: 'The one with the glass front'
  3 **C**: '… and it's the second door on the left?'

Recognizing repetition and avoiding distractors p. 8

1 Keiko repeats the directions back to Stephen for confirmation.
2 In the last extract, Stephen replied 'That's right!' He means, 'You are correct', but if you are not listening carefully, you might think that the <u>door</u> is on the right.

Completing notes p. 8

1 1 think carefully
  2 near (to) home
  3 study abroad/overseas

3 1 *$130*: 'That's $130 per week, or $90 without meals.' $90 is incorrect because this is the price without meals.

2 *college halls/halls of residence/college residential block*: 'There are three kinds of accommodation that we deal with – home stays, college halls of residence, or private lets.' The instructions do not state that you should use words from the text, so you can use your own, and in this case, you have to as *college halls of residence* is four words and would be incorrect. *College halls residence* is also incorrect as it is ungrammatical.
3 *reasonably priced/fairly priced*: '… but we make sure that you are paying a reasonable price.' You need to change the words from the text to make grammatical sense.

5 4 Jenkins
  5 British
  6 562, Green Park Road
  7 07785 265 981

Listening for numbers and letters p. 9

4 1 *Sir Anthony Winton.* Make sure you can spell *Mr, Mrs, Miss, Ms* and *Sir.*
  2 *34.92.* Numbers after the decimal point are always said individually, eg *point nine two*, not *point ninety-two.*
  3 *15 Sparrow Lane.* Make sure you can spell words like *Lane.*
  4 *29,030* (feet)
  5 *Michael MacWilliams.* There is another capital letter after *Mc* or *Mac.*
  6 *286 Banbury Road.* Abbreviations for *road* (Rd) and *street* (St) are acceptable.
  7 *74%*
  8 *Janet Gates*
  9 *0121 6749544.* All numbers are said separately, except for *double 4*, and there is a pause between each set of numbers.
  10 *654/120084* (/ is usually pronounced *forward slash*)
  11 *Mrs J Robson-Smith.* If someone has two surnames, there is a hyphen between them.
  12 *Flat 3, 547 Oxford Road*
  13 *www. bht.co.uk* (. is pronounced *dot* in web addresses)
  14 *Dr. Brown*
  15 N 770 CES. Numbers are pronounced separately for ID/registration numbers.

Skills practice p. 10

1 C
2 D
3 set menu/three course meal
4 vegetarian/made without meat
5 coffee/cappuccino or espresso
6 12
7 £25
8 (Mr) (Dan) Glover
9 01452 863092

Using key words for prediction p. 11

1 1 **A** gives information about used car sales. (eg second-hand cars)
  B tells you the best way to buy a car. (eg most efficient/most effective)
  C tells you the most popular way to sell a car. (Note that this is talking about selling, while the others mention buying a car.)
  D looks at different ways of buying a new car. (This answer is the only one that specifies new cars.)
 2 **A** You are a new driver. (eg you have just passed your test)
  B You have had an accident in your old car. (Listen for words like crash or smash.)
  C You don't have a lot of money. (Listen for cheap or inexpensive.)
  D Your old car is unreliable. (Maybe it often breaks down.)
  E You want to learn to drive. (eg you want driving lessons)
 3 **A** they have a lot of room to show you the cars. (eg there is a lot of space)
  B they are cheap. (or inexpensive)
  C you have a legal right to return the car if something goes wrong. (eg a warranty/guarantee)
  D they are honest. (eg they are trustworthy/they won't cheat you)

2   Eliminating wrong answers p. 11

 1 **A** CORRECT. 'Today we're going to talk about the different ways there are of buying a used car …'
  B INCORRECT. Not 'the best way' but 'the different ways' of buying a car.
  C INCORRECT. The recording specifies 'of *buying* a used car.'
  D INCORRECT. The recording talks about used cars, not new cars.
 2 **A** CORRECT. The recording says, '… maybe you've just passed your test …'
  B INCORRECT. Nothing is mentioned about an accident.
  C CORRECT. The recording says, 'You look at new cars but they are so expensive …'
  D CORRECT. The recording says, 'So your old car has broken down again …'
  E INCORRECT. If you had a car before, or have just passed your test, you already know how to drive.
  F INCORRECT. This is not mentioned.
   Note: with this type of question, if you choose fewer answers than you are asked for, even if they are correct you will <u>not</u> get <u>any</u> marks.
 3 **A** INCORRECT. The place where cars are sold is called a *showroom*.
  B INCORRECT. Dealers are usually about £800–£1,000 more expensive.
  C CORRECT. If something goes wrong with the car after you've bought it, you can take it back.
  D INCORRECT. This isn't mentioned.

Completing a summary p. 11

1 1 This must be an adjective such as *good/better/safe(r)/cheap(er)*, etc.
 2 This must be a noun: what kind of things can you look through?
 3 The article tells us that this must be a noun.
 4 The answer to this is probably a person or a time.
 5 This must be a noun: what will you not have at an auction?

2 **Note**: there is often more than one acceptable answer to these questions, because the question doesn't state that you have to use words from the text.
 1 *cheaper/less expensive* 'If you're looking for a cheaper car …'
 2 *(local) papers/adverts* '… by looking in the adverts in your local paper.'
 3 *(obvious) problem/disadvantage/difficulty* 'The obvious problem is that once you've bought the car it's yours and you can't really take it back.'
 4 *by a mechanic/before you buy* '… get a mechanic to check it over for you before you buy it.'
 5 *time* '… you won't really have time to check the car over.'

Skills practice p. 12

1 C
2 B
3 B and E (you MUST have both of these)
4 travel insurance
5 (quite) expensive
6 get home/back
7 too much sun/the (midday) sun
8 clean your teeth/have *or* use ice
9 liquids/fluids/soft drinks/bottled water

Listening for specific speakers p. 13

1 There are three speakers. They greet each other by name.
2 Robert, Anand and Claire.
3 Robert and Claire speak twice. Anand speaks three times.

Listening for specific information/short answers p. 13

1 Qu 2 What is the <u>word limit</u> for the assignment? This must be a number. Qu 3 <u>Where</u> did Robert get his idea for a topic from? This must be a location or a situation: where might you get an idea?

2 1 **A** *water pollution*
   B *global warming*
   'Oh, you know, <u>water pollution</u> like the oil tanker that broke up and killed all the sea life for miles near Spain, or the kind of thing that's always talked about, like <u>global warming</u>.'
 2 *2, 000 words*
   Robert: What's the <u>word limit</u>, again? Is it 1,500 words, as usual?
   Anand: No, this one's 500 words longer.
   Claire: <u>2,000</u>? Help! We've got more work that I thought!
 3 *an Internet search/the Internet*. 'Have you got any <u>ideas for a topic</u>?' 'I looked through books in the library and some journals, but what worked in the end was <u>an Internet search</u>.'

Completing a table p. 13

1 Questions 1 and 4 ask you to identify the types of pollution. Question 2 must be a date.

2

Pollution problem	Solution provided by	Date completed
(1) *Sewage*	City Council	**(2)** *1970s*
Boat traffic	**(3)** *State government*	next year
(4) *Rubbish*	**(5)** *(Local) divers/ diving clubs*	ongoing project

Classifying p. 14

1

Sea creatures	Stormy weather	Sewage	Emissions
crab	*rain and wind*	*waste water*	*jetski/motor boat fuel*
marine life	*blown*		

3 1 **R** 'I think that they leave the rubbish if any marine life has started living in it – they wouldn't want to make a crab homeless!

2 **S** 'When the weather is bad, especially if there's a lot of rain and a wind blowing towards the shore, the sewage can still be blown in to the beaches.'

3 **B** 'Emissions are actually getting worse …'

4 **S** '… actually, they get much more bothered when they have to swim in waste water, after a storm …'

Spelling p. 14

1 and **2**

1 *site* (NOT *sight*). Take care with words that have more than one meaning and spelling, but which sound the same.

2 *6th February.* The month MUST begin with a capital letter.

3 *Wednesday.* Days of the week MUST begin with a capital letter.

4 *suggest*

5 *inexpensive.* Take care with prefixes.

6 *Unemployment*

7 *advise* (NOT *advice*). Note that the sound is different, and here a verb is needed.

8 *politician* (NOT *polititian*). Take care with *-ion* endings.

9 *companies.* Take care with the plural, especially irregular plurals or those which take *-ies*.

10 *successful.* Remember *full* has double *l*, but the suffix only has one *l*.

11 *independent.* Take care with *-ent/-ant* endings.

12 *Receiving.* Take care with the order of *i* and *e*.

3 *constant*, *perceived* and *sufficient* were spelt wrongly.

Skills practice p. 15

	'A' Levels	Foundation Course
Length of course	2 years	1 year
Number of subjects studied	2–3	**(1)** *1*
English language support given	often none	**(2)** *6 hours* per *week*
Main type of assessment	exam(s)	**(3)** *continual assessment or assignments and presentations*
Most popular with	**(4)** *British students*	overseas students

5 academic 9 M
6 essay structure/essays 10 A
7 global markets 11 M
8 It sounds hard/difficult 12 P

Labelling a diagram with numbered parts p. 16

1 1 *Diagram 1*: shows a process. It's a good idea to think about where the process starts and what the most important parts of the process are.
Diagram 2: shows an object. Parts of an object will usually be described in relation to each other, so think about which parts are next to, above or below each other.
Diagram 3: shows a map. For plans, think about which way the plan is orientated, and where features like doors, staircases, etc. are. For maps, look for roads, buildings, rivers, etc.

2 **Diagram 1**
A *light rays.* '… light rays from the object, … come through the lens …'
B *virtual image.* '… sees a virtual image, which is closer and smaller than the real object.'
Diagram 2
A *face.* '… on the front of the clock, we call this the *clock face* …'
B *pendulum.* '… and behind that, the *pendulum.* That's P-E-N-D-U-L-U-M.'
C *weight.* '… driven by a weight, which is situated in front of the pendulum …'
Diagram 3
A *cafeteria.* '… and the cafeteria is right behind it. You can get to the cafeteria through the Students' Union, or through a separate entrance at the back.'
B *(a large) lawn.* 'If you walk out of the main entrance to the Union, there is a large lawn area …'
C *library.* '… to your left is the library …'

3 Diagram shows a hydroelectric plant. A is behind the dam; B is under the ground; C is under the dam; D joins the plant and leads away from it.

4 A *reservoir*. '... a large artificial lake, called a reservoir. That's R-E-S-E-R-V-O-I-R.'

B *turbine*. 'The turbine is situated underground. Sorry, what was that? Turbine, T-U-R-B-I-N-E.'

C *control gate*. '... under the dam there is a control gate and this can be opened to let the water in.'

D *power lines*. '... by the power lines, shown leading away from the power station.'

Labelling a flow chart p. 17

1 and 2

1   100,000 v
2   power distribution
3   (normal) domestic (electric)
4   (electrical) accidents/accidents with electricity

Sentence completion p. 17

1 1   You need adjectives to complete these gaps. What kind of positive adjectives could be used about hydroelectricity?

2   You need a noun here. What kind of factors limit hydroelectricity?

2 1   *clean/green, little pollution caused* or *sustainable* '... it is a very clean and green method ... and it's sustainable ...'

2   *(a large) river/reliable water (flow)* '... obviously a large river is needed with a reliable flow of water ...'

Listening for signpost words p. 17

1   A. This phrase is used after the speaker has recapped on previously given information, before the speaker moves on to add further, related information.

2   B. In this context, the speaker is drawing attention to a visual, but this could also be used to emphasize a point.

3   C. If this phrase is used, the information that follows is usually related to what went before, but not usually contrasting it.

Skills practice p. 18

1   600 million
2   sediment/sand and mud
3   heat
4   sandstone/limestone (NOT reservoir rock)
5   oil
6   faulting
7   cap rock
8   (access) roads
9   water
10 reserve pit
11 (the) main hole
12 brought in

Quiz p.19

1   B
2   B
3   C
4   A
5   A magazines, B newspapers, E advertisements, F leaflets. (C reports + D case studies are in the Academic test)
6   False. (unlike the Listening module)
7   True. The texts in section 2 are related to tertiary education and training.
8   False. (there are a variety of question types, including multiple choice, short answer questions, completing sentences/notes/charts/diagrams, matching, classifying, etc.)
9   True. The text will probably be an article from a magazine or newspaper and so the organization, structure and language will be more complicated.

Short-answer questions p.20

1   *pain and fever*
2   *(in) liquid form*
3   *immunization*
4   *pregnant women*
5   *eight/8 tablets*
6   *six/6 hourly*

Skills practice p.21

Paraphrasing p.21

1   a
2   a
3   b
4   a
5   b
6   b

Matching headings to paragraphs p.23

ix Work out what you can afford

A You have decided to move into a flat. <u>The first thing you need to do is your sums</u> – before you commit to anything. As an example, <u>if your rent is $120 per week, then you may need 4 weeks' rent as bond and 2 weeks' rent in advance. That's $720 in total</u> before you even move in.

iv What to do after you've asked around

B <u>Often friends or colleagues know of a vacant place</u> but otherwise there are other things to try. <u>Read through the "To Let" column</u> in your local newspaper. You could <u>put an advertisement</u> in the window of your local corner shop saying that you are flat-hunting and leaving your contact details. Some <u>real estate agents also have rental flats available.</u>

vii Make sure the arrangement is in writing

C Once you've found a flat, you should get a <u>tenancy agreement, which is a contract between you, the tenant*, and the landlord.</u> It sets out what you and your landlord each agree to do. Every tenancy agreement must be <u>signed by both you and the landlord,</u> with a copy held by each of you.

iii Sorting out financial agreements

D You and the landlord will <u>work out when, where and how you'll pay the rent</u>. The landlord must give you a receipt for the rent you pay. If you are using automatic payments or a not-negotiable personal cheque, the bank records act as receipts. You will usually be asked to pay rent in advance

v Your legal position once you're in the flat

E If you are a flatmate rather than a tenant, you may have <u>different rights. Tenants are responsible to the landlord for the whole of the rent and any damage done.</u> If you have an agreement with a landlord, you're a tenant. If someone signs the agreement and then allows you to share the flat you are a flatmate. <u>Only landlords can ask tenants to leave, but a flatmate can be asked by the tenant.</u>

viii Sorting out disagreements

F Should you have any <u>problems regarding your tenancy,</u> you can contact *Tenancy Services*. They will provide you with advice about your rights and obligations and you can then decide on the next step to take. If you <u>cannot resolve the matter with the landlord, their trained mediators will try and help you both settle the dispute.</u>

i The tenant's responsibilities

G It is <u>up to you to pay the rent on time</u> and <u>keep the premises reasonably clean and tidy.</u> You must <u>notify the landlord</u> as soon as <u>any repairs are needed.</u> You <u>should not exceed the number of occupants stated in the tenancy agreement.</u>

Skills practice p.23

Skimming to find the general theme p.23

A=ii Changes to payments
B=iii Make sure the flat suits your needs
C=i The facilities you should expect

Vocabulary development p.23

1	right	7	neighbours
2	amount	8	find out/enquire
3	fortnightly	9	find out/know/enquire
4	alter	10	permitted
5	set up	11	provide
6	finding out/knowing/ enquiring	12	fully furnished
		13	higher

Multiple matching: Matching options to extract p.24

1 It is necessary to buy tickets before the day of the event.
   C <u>Cookery class</u>
   Ying Zhang Xue is head chef at the Canton Café. For just £5, he will show you how to prepare some delicious and nutritious dishes. Thursday 12th 7.30 p.m. Room 3 ***Tickets must be purchased in advance at reception.***

2 It is not recommended that children attend this event.
   E *On the beach*
   Written by Craig Bailey, this play deals with childhood experience and adult memories. **Violent scenes mean it is unsuitable for children**. Opening night is Friday 21st (8 p.m.) before a national tour begins. Tickets on sale now (£20). The Hall

3 It is suitable for different levels of ability.

B <u>Yoga</u>
   This class continues to run at these times:
   Beginners Tuesdays 7–8 p.m.
   Intermediate Wednesdays 7.30–8.30 p.m.
   Advanced Saturdays 10–11 a.m.
   £6 for an hour's class. All ages welcome. (Crèche available for children) Bring towel and bottle of water. Room 3

4 It costs nothing to attend this event.
   G <u>Summerfield – a history</u>
   Local historian Jenny Grove will give **a free talk and slide show** on the history of our town. Copies of Grove's book *Reflections* (£25) will be on sale afterwards. Wednesday 26th 8 p.m. Room 3.

5 It will happen again if enough people like it.
   A <u>Bang the Drum!</u>
   The first time this music class is being offered to children in Summerfield.
   No booking necessary – just turn up! **If popular, it will become a regular class**. £2 per child. Monday 2nd 10 a.m.–11 a.m. Room 2

6 It may have to take place in another location.
   F <u>Concert</u>
   Enjoy an unforgettable evening of traditional blues music from *Days Gone By*. The band has performed to audiences all over the country. **If the good weather lasts, the concert will be in the Community Centre garden. Otherwise it will take place in the hall.** Sunday 23rd 6 p.m. Tickets £10

Recognizing part of speech p.25

Noun	Verb	Adjective	Adverb
popularity	to popularize smthg	popular	popularly
regularity	to regularize smthg	regular	regularly
a delicacy		delicious	
nutrition a nutritionist nutrient		nutritious	nutritiously
a nation	to nationalize smthg	national	nationally
a tradition a traditionalist		traditional	traditionally
violence		violent	violently
difference	to differentiate between two things	different	differently
suitability	to suit s.o/smthg	(un)suitable	suitably
forgetfulness	to forget s.o/smthg	(un) forgettable forgetful	unforgettably forgetfully
freedom	to free s.o	free	freely
necessity	to necessitate smthg	necessary	necessarily

Guessing the meaning from context p.26

a   destination = the place you are traveling to
b   to en+able you = to make you able
c   informed = adj   information = n   a decision you made after you got enough information
d   co = together. A negative meaning because of environmental destruction + causing problems. colluding = participating in
e   object = v   to strongly disagree with something/to be against something
f   refrain = v   to stop yourself doing something
g   fragile = adj   something which is fragile can easily be broken or damaged
h   erosion = n   the slow destruction/disappearance of the earth/ground
i   designated = adj   to design = v   a designated area is an area which has been designed or marked out for a purpose/reason
j   to en+sure = to make sure

Matching options to paragraphs/sections p.26

1   **the reason why some people do not need to take the whole driving test**
D   Some countries require similar driving skills and have similar licensing systems to New Zealand's so drivers from these countries may not have to sit the practical driving test. If your licence comes from Australia, Canada, Norway, a member state of the European Union, South Africa, Switzerland or the United States of America, you don't have to sit the practical test.
2   **an example of how driving rules are different in New Zealand.**
C   All drivers must know the road regulations and signs. Learning these is particularly important because of our unique 'Give Way' regulation (you must give way to vehicles coming from the opposite direction and turning right, when you are turning left). You can find out more about this when you study the Road Code.
3   **the conditions that need to be fulfilled before someone can work as a driver**
B   If you want to earn a living from driving you will probably need to convert to a New Zealand driver licence first and then get a driver licence endorsement. For example, you have to complete courses, pass exams and have a police check before you can earn money carrying passengers or drive a truck.
4   **behaviour that could lead to a person's licence being taken away**
H   Roadside Licence Suspension means the police seize a driver's licence and immediately suspend them from driving for 28 days. This can happen if you are caught driving at more than double the legal alcohol limit or are caught speeding at more than 50km/h above the limit
5   **the procedure required if someone is believed to have a certain disability**
G   Your eyesight will be checked when you apply for a new licence. An eyesight machine will check how well you can see at a distance and to the sides. If the check detects a problem you will need to present an eyesight or medical certificate before your licence can be issued.
6   **a restriction on what kind of vehicle a person is allowed to drive**
A   If you have an overseas driver licence or international driving permit you can drive for one year after you first arrive in New Zealand. If you do not have one of these you must apply for a New Zealand driver licence. You can only drive the types of vehicles covered by your overseas driver licence or international driving permit.

Skills practice

Multiple-matching tasks p.28

1   a **means/a way** of obtaining animals for zoos
d   Many animals are captured by hunters in their natural habitat and shipped across the world to a different continent.
2   **conditions** that zoos must fulfil to take care of their animals
c   Zoos must ensure the living areas of their animals are large enough for them to explore and clean enough for them to remain healthy.
3   an **explanation** for the popularity of zoos
a   Nowadays we have access to exotic animals through television documentaries but in the past, the only way people could experience them was by a visit to the zoo – an exciting day out for the whole family
4   a **disadvantage**/a **drawback** of not having zoos
b   If many zoos do close down, it will mean that far fewer people will have the chance to have close contact with exotic animals.
5   an **improvement** that zoos have made
f   Over the last few decades, many cages have been replaced by larger enclosures which provide the animals with a more natural environment.
6   a **justification** for the existence of zoos
g   It is often said that without zoos many animals themselves would no longer survive. In the wild, they would have been hunted to extinction.
7   **evidence** of the bad effect zoos have on animal behaviour
h   You can still see animals pacing backwards and forwards along the same path for hours. Some animals pull out their own fur while other animals refuse to eat.
8   a **procedure** for releasing animals into their natural environment
e   Zoo-born chimpanzees cannot simply be let free to go back into the wild. First they are taken to a huge enclosure at the edge of the forest. Here they need to learn how to find food for themselves and build their own nests. Human contact is reduced every day.

True/False/Not Given p.29

1   NG   The text only tells us about who can use the computers and what the students can use the computers for. It doesn't mention anything about booking.
2   F   The text says that students can get help from reception whenever they want, but they will only learn the name of their personal counsellor on Orientation Day.
3   T   The text says that students from various (different/other) colleges can post (put up) notices (advertisements) for people to share an apartment (flatmates).
4   NG   The text only says that it is possible for students to stay at hotels. It does not mention the possibility of the college making a booking.
5   F   The text says that the college can get insurance with BC Medical Services for students but they will not be able to use this insurance for three months. ('this coverage will not take effect for three months')

6 T The text says that students who are staying with college homestay families *and* students who are staying in alternative (other) accommodation can be collected from the airport.

7 NG The text says that Canada Swan Travel can help students to book flights and give them information on trips and tours. It does not mention that it can help them to get a visa as well.

Skills practice p.30

Section 2 Vocabulary p.30

1

a campus
b lecture room
c financial division
d accommodation
e college admissions
f careers service
g self-access centre
h canteen
i health and safety

Sentence completion p.30

1 G **The cost of a course depends on the programme a student takes.**
Students wishing to attend the college are required to pay for tuition, administration costs and materials for each year of their course. The fee is calculated according to the particular programme they intend to follow.

2 I **No refund will be given for the first-year enrolment fees.**
A NZ$175 enrolment fee is also required for international students, but this is a one-time payment for their first year only. If students decide to cancel or withdraw from a course, they may receive a refund of tuition fees but the enrolment fee is non-refundable.

3 F **Students can expect to receive refunds according to the date the application is received.**
Should a student wish and be entitled to claim a tuition refund, the date we receive their application is the date used to calculate the amount, rather than the last day of the student's attendance on the course. Students are advised that they should receive their refund no later than 4 weeks after the application has been submitted.

4 B **Confirmation of enrolment depends on the complete payment of every fee.**
To guarantee a place on a course, students need to pay all fees in full by the deadline stated in their acceptance letter. If this condition is not met, students will not be enrolled.

5 H **The amount of additional tuition fees is based on the extra credit points a student can gain.**
In order to obtain a student permit from the immigration service, students must be studying a course which amounts to no less than 120 credit points per year, or 60 per term. Should a course the student intends to take be worth more than 120 credits, further tuition fees will be payable depending on the number of extra credit points it provides.

6 C **There is no additional charge for the language classes the college provides.**
Students wishing to apply for pre-course English language classes should note that no fee is required.

However, students will have to pay for any external examination they take in this subject.

Skills practice p.31

Section 2 vocabulary p.31

a to apply for : this means you send a letter or complete a form when you want to get a job/a loan/a scholarship/a place on a course, etc.
to enrol on : you enrol on a course or a study programme after you are offered a place. It means that you put your name on the list of course participants and (usually) pay your course fees.

b costs: money that is spent on rent, electricity, producing documents, advertising
fees: money you pay to attend a course or to pay for a professional service, for example, to a doctor or a lawyer

c to cancel: when you cancel something, for example, a meeting/a course/an appointment, you decide that it will not happen.
to postpone: when you postpone something, for example, a meeting/a course/an appointment, you decide that it will happen at a later date.

d to attend: you can attend a course/a programme/a lesson – this means you only listen to the teacher or lecturer. You can also attend a meeting – which means you both listen and contribute to the meeting, and you can attend college – this means you are a student at the college.
to participate in: if you participate in a lesson or a meeting, you offer your ideas and opinions

e a condition: you can find conditions in a contract or an agreement, for example: you can attend a course if you pay for it in advance, or you can receive a student loan if you are unemployed.
a rule: an organization or an institution may have a set of rules they expect people to follow, for example: You cannot smoke in this building, or To use the computers in the self-access room, you need to write your name on the booking form.

f a refund: to receive a refund means to receive the money back that you paid for a product or service.
a receipt: when you pay for a product or service, you receive a small piece of paper which shows what the product/service is/ the date + time it was bought/the cost/the place it was bought. You often need to show your receipt if you want a refund.
There is also an expression which is used in formal writing : on receipt of : for example:
We will send you the books on receipt of payment = we will send you the books when we have received payment.

g a permit: a permit is an official document that shows you are allowed to do something or be somewhere eg a work permit, a permit to stay in a foreign country, a parking permit
permission: you are given permission when someone tells you that you are allowed to do something eg to give someone permission to have a day off work, to give in an essay on a later date.

Sentence completion without a choice of possible answers p.32

1 (valuable) work experience
2 skills and abilities
3 academic qualifications
4 aptitude
5 terms and conditions
6 deposit

Skills practice p.33

Section 2 Vocabulary p.33

1

1 submit, assignments
2 situated
3 designed
4 are entitled to
5 get a discount on
6 criteria, gain entry to
7 select, staff members, up-to-date
8 Job-seekers
9 evaluated

2

1 further education
2 living costs
3 application process
4 intensive training
5 foundation course
6 selection procedure
7 academic performance
8 work experience

Matching p.34

1 C **People's brains are more challenged now than they used to be.**
But Professor Marois said that a VSTM capacity of four was probably not much of a problem in the relatively slower-paced lives of our hunter-gatherer ancestors. But the stressful pace of modern life, he says, is stretching our Stone Age brains to the limit. (lines 109–115)

2 D **It's possible that people with good visual memories are also clear thinkers.**
According to Professor Brian Butterworth, this visual memory may also be linked to intelligence. In the same way that a computer with a large working memory can tackle problems more quickly, people with a greater capacity for holding images in their heads may have better reasoning and problem-solving skills. (lines 73–80)

3 A **Concentration on one subject may prevent people from noticing other details in a scene.**
It shows, he says, that when people are really focused on something, they can be 'blind' to other features in the background. However, if people were simply asked to view the tape, they noticed the gorilla easily. (lines 43–47)

4 C **People tend to overestimate their ability to accurately remember visual details,**
"Although we have the impression we are taking in a great deal of information from a visual scene, we are actually very poor at describing it in detail once it is gone from our sight," said Professor Marois. (lines 64–68)

5 A **People do not always notice significant change in visual detail**
In one experiment, people who were walking across a college campus were asked by a stranger for directions. During the resulting conversation, two men carrying a wooden door passed between the stranger and the subject*. After the door went by, the subject was asked if they had been surprised by anything. Half of those tested failed to notice that, as the door passed by, a shorter, darker man was in the stranger's place. Sure enough, although the subjects had talked to the stranger for 10–15 seconds before the swap, Simons discovered that half of them were not aware that, after the passing of the door, they had ended up speaking to another person. (lines 16–31)

6 B **Our poor ability to remember details may result in accidents on the road.**
This memory limitation could contribute to traffic accidents, said Dr Vogel, because of the need to maintain and monitor information about other cars, pedestrians and cyclists. "While this hasn't been tested directly, it seems highly plausible that racing drivers have higher VSTM capacity than normal drivers." (lines 94–101)

Summary with choice of possible answers p.35

1 limited
2 aware
3 focused
4 capable
5 logical
6 stressful

Global multiple choice p.36

D

Skills practice p.36

Understanding ideas p.36

1 b it emphasizes the truth of the previous sentence
2 you cannot say that your brain never deceives you
3 it is possible to see something without observing it
4 people/subjects who were
5 Despite the fact that/Even though
6 the fact that people do not always notice significant details
7 The 'gorilla' test that Dr Simons carried out
8 a it is followed by a comparison.

Classification p.36

1 B **there is no good reason for children to be on a low-salt diet**
If you're young and don't suffer from hypertension, there's not much evidence to support a low-salt diet, and there seems no case at all for restricting the table salt intake of children, except perhaps to get them accustomed to a low-salt diet that might benefit them in middle age.

2 C **some companies have deliberately misled people about the effects of salt**
The writer does not say anything about the way companies have presented salt to the public.

3 A **a lack of iodine is dangerous for pregnant women**
In pregnant women, iodine deficiency can cause serious harm to the baby's health.

4　B　**salt use has been decreasing since the 1990s in New Zealand**
The children were studied in the late 90s, so it's probable that salt use has declined even more since then

5　A　**a health campaign has led to illness in New Zealand**
The campaign against salt has been so successful that New Zealand is now experiencing an epidemic of goitre, an enlargement of the thyroid gland which causes swelling in the throat, usually found in much poorer countries. …

6　A　**an increase of potassium in the diet is more significant than a reduction in salt**
However, a 1997 study called DASH (Dietary Approaches to Stop Hypertension) – demonstrated that a potassium*-rich diet of fruit, vegetables, whole grains, nuts and low-fat dairy products substantially reduced blood pressure, even when salt intake remained the same.

7　C　**the health benefits of salt depends on the way it has been refined**
The writer does not say anything about the way salt can be refined.

8　A　**children in New Zealand are not getting enough iodine nowadays**
A study of 300 eight to ten year old New Zealand children in the late 1990s found that 11.3% showed signs of iodine deficiency, having thyroids greater in size than the upper limit for their ages

Multiple-matching p.37

A,C,D,E
A　a way of preventing infections = Soldiers often died from minor wounds because there was no salt for disinfectants.
C　a supplement to the diet of animals = Like humans, animals need salt and seek out brine springs or rock salt, which they lick. Farmers must provide their livestock with salt when they cannot seek it out for themselves.
D　a way of keeping food fresh = … because salt is added to everything from bread to baked beans, for taste or to aid preservation or both.
E　a means of payment = In Roman times, soldiers were sometimes paid in salt, hence the origin of the word 'salary'.

Global p.37

D

Recognizing the writer's attitude p.39

Approval
It's time that we
It would be no bad thing if the government
I am in full agreement with the proposal
We must back
I am in favour of

Disapproval
It hardly seems fair
I am against
I object to
I feel we should resist
It's my belief that we should make a stand against
I am strongly opposed to

Strong possibility
It hardly seems likely that
In all likelihood,
There is little doubt that
In all probability,
It's fairly certain that

Doubt
It is questionable whether
One has to be sceptical about whether
It's doubtful whether …

Expectation
Predictably, they found that
It came as no surprise to find that
Indeed, they found that
Just as they had anticipated,

Surprise
In fact, they found that
They could not have foreseen that
They actually found that

Yes/No/Not Given p.40

1　YES　Parents today are not surprised when their children return home.
In the modern take on this theme, sure, the parents … would hardly find it remarkable when their kids turned up on the doorstep having squandered the job, the flat, the partner and the loan. The return of grown children to the family house has become commonplace.

2　NOT GIVEN　American children who return home have respect for their parents.
The writer only mentions the percentage of children who return home – not their attitude towards their parents.

3　YES　Men and women may share the same reasons for returning home.
For a man, the return to cooked meals, a laundry service and maternal love is regarded as a refusal to grow up. However, by no means is this reluctance only a masculine trait.

4　NOT GIVEN　Parents expect children who return home to make a financial contribution.
The writer does not mention that parents expect their children to give them money. Mary Bold says children should pay rent, but the writer does not support this.

5　NO　The suggestions that Mary Bold makes should work well for most families.
The writer rejects Mary Bold's theories. She insists there are various conditions to 'make a re-filled nest work well'. Some of these seem straightforward, if not necessarily easy; others impossible to monitor and enforce. According to Bold, 'boomerangers' must pay rent , they need to get along with mum, they can only return once, their return must be regarded as a safety net only, they must be good company. In real life, no-one is that structured.

6　YES　Dave Hendl blames himself for his son's lack of independence.
And guess what? It's all down to the parents. "We probably should have forced responsibility on to the kids and made them more aware of the value of looking after themselves."

7　NO　Young people nowadays believe it should be unnecessary to work as hard as their parents did.
They expect to struggle for the milestones that former generations took for granted – a degree, a career path, a house, a pension.

Locating information p.40

1   **E   the idea of mature or immature behaviour not depending on age.**
    When does one become an adult? Byrd says "Age boundaries are not numbers. In public, people might be treated as adults, might be adults, but, at home all of a sudden you're treated and you might act as though you're fourteen. <u>Then it's not so much about age boundaries as about your attitude towards those you interact with.</u>"

2   **A   the idea of young people returning home being a historical one.**
    There are <u>a number of cultures which share a similar fable; that of the ambitious child who leaves home and then suddenly returns</u>, a failure. The astonished parents are simply relieved they are safe and back home

3   **G   an explanation that supports the behaviour of children who do not leave home.**
    … but their decision to trade impoverished independence for higher purchasing power has a <u>certain</u> depressing <u>rationality</u>. They expect to struggle for.. a degree, a career path, a house, a pension. At the same time, they want they want immediate job fulfillment and a satisfying social life. <u>So it makes sense</u> to exact a sort of retribution by continuing to be a burden on the family. This contradiction between continued dependence and the desire for autonomy might seem adolescent. <u>But perhaps that's the point. Boomerang kids' unwillingness to leave adolescence mirrors the baby boomers' increasingly frantic attempts to stay young.</u>

4   **C   the fact that young people enjoy spending their money on what they want.**
    Other theories blame <u>materialism</u> and a lack of maturity among the pampered young. The ever-receding average marriage age might be the reason why so many singles are sitting at home, but <u>consumerism</u> appears to compensate amply for their lack of a spouse. Back in the family home, <u>they have the option to treat nearly all of their earnings as disposable income.</u>

5   **B   evidence that the modern trend of children returning home is not limited to one culture.**
    Who says you can never go back? … 'boomerang children' or 'boomerangs' in English-speaking countries are 'parasite singles' in Japan and 'mama's boys' in Italy. Figures from the US suggest that 18 million Americans aged 18–34 live with their parents –about one third of the age group. Of this lot, 4.5 million are over 25. UK statistics show the same pattern

Global p.40

D

Skills practice p.42

Understanding the writer's purpose p.42

a   to describe
b   to discuss
c   to contrast
d   to summarize
e   to introduce

Section 3

Multiple choice p.42

1   **D   have adapted to a human environment.**
    Vilmos Csányi's department is full of canines: dogs are in the hall, in the classroom and working in the laboratories where Mr. Csányi and his colleagues are trying to determine just how much their brains are capable of. There are no cages at Loránd Eötvös University's department of ethology, the study of animal behavior. And why would there be? asks Mr. Csányi, the department's founder and chairman. In adjusting to our world, <u>Mr. Csányi argues, our best friends have acquired a remarkable number of mental characteristics that closely resemble our own.</u> His team has been studying canine cognition* for the past decade and has evidence that suggests dogs have far greater mental capabilities than scientists have previously believed. "Our experiments indicate a high level of social understanding in dogs," he says. <u>And in their relationship with humans, dogs have developed remarkable interspecies-communications skills. "They easily accept a membership in the family, they provide and request information, and are able to cooperate and imitate human actions,"</u> he says.

2   **B   People who are not dog owners can often understand what dogs mean.**
    The latest findings to come out of the department suggest that dogs' barks have evolved into a relatively sophisticated way of communicating with humans. Adam Miklósi, an ethology professor, set out to see if humans can interpret what dogs mean when they bark. He recruited 90 human volunteers and played them 21 recordings of barking Hungarian mudis, a breed* of dog that herd sheep. The recordings captured dogs in seven situations, such as playing with other dogs, anticipating food, and encountering a human intruder. <u>The people showed strong agreement about the emotional meaning of the various barks, regardless of whether they owned a mudi or another breed, or had never owned a dog. Owners and nonowners were also just as successful at deducing the situation that had elicited the barks, guessing correctly in a third of the situations, or about double the rate of chance.</u>

3   **B   Domesticated dogs require permission before they will perform an action.**
    In scientific circles, animal-cognition studies have focused on animals such as chimpanzees. And until recently, dogs were also thought to be intellectually inferior to wolves. A study published in 1985 by Harry Frank, a psychologist at the University of Michigan, showed that wolves could unlock a complicated gate mechanism after watching a human do it once, while dogs remained confused, even after considerable exposure. This led some scientists to conclude that dogs' intellectual capacity diminished during domestication*. <u>But Csányi suspected that dogs were simply more inhibited than their wild cousins, requiring a signal from their masters before opening a gate.</u> So eight years ago, he conducted a problem-solving experiment of his own. With their masters present, 28 dogs of various ages, breeds, and levels of training had to figure out how to pull on handles of plastic dishes to obtain meat on the other side of a wire fence. <u>Regardless of other factors, the dogs with the strongest relationship with</u>

their owner scored worst, continually seeking approval or assistance. The best results came from outdoor dogs, who obtained the meat, on average, in one-third the time. Most telling, when owners were allowed to signal approval, the gap between indoor and outdoor dogs vanished.

4 C Unlike chimpanzees, dogs know when a person is unaware of something.

To find out, Mr. Csányi went to the homes of Budapest's many dog owners. After introducing the researchers to the dogs, the owners would leave the room. Then the dogs would watch Mr. Csányi hide a piece of food somewhere inaccessible to them. When the owners returned, the dogs would run or glance back and forth from master to hiding place, clearly signaling its location. More recent experiments substituted nonfood objects and had similar results, which suggests the dogs may be placing themselves in their owner's shoes, and realizing that the humans are ignorant of the object's location. Similar tests on chimpanzees has not found evidence of the same skills.

5 A Researchers do not always consider what can influence an experiment.

Not everyone agrees with their findings. Raymond P. Coppinger, a dog cognition specialist, is concerned that researchers like Csányi are failing to properly control experiments for the "Clever Hans effect," named after a horse that tapped out the answers to mathematical problems more than a century ago. Although people at the time were amazed at Hans' ability, scientists later concluded that the horse was picking up unintentional cues from the person who posed the question. Hans was clever enough to figure out that he would get a treat if he stopped tapping when the human in front of him subtly reacted to the arrival of the 'correct answer'; the horse didn't actually know arithmetic.
And Michael J. Owren, assistant professor of psychology at Cornell University, will also not go so far as the Hungarians in crediting dogs with relatively high cognitive skills. He says Mr. Csányi's team may be underestimating the flexibility of associative learning, the most basic kind of learning that comes not from "thinking" out the problem, but simply by associating events or objects with one another. "Dogs are supremely sensitive to cues being produced by humans and are able to interact with humans very effectively," Mr. Owren says. " Csányi's team are using pet-class dogs who have been socialized in a very unique way," adds Coppinger. "To be talking about dogs in general when you are only referring to this small population which have been bred for all sorts of specific tasks is going to mislead

Summary p.43

6 (high) cognitive skills
7 events or objects
8 cues
9 interaction
10 pet-class
11 (specific) tasks
12 + 13   B+E

Skills practice p.43

1 Colons can be followed by a paraphrase, an explanation or a list.

In a, you can understand the meaning of *canines* because the writer writes the information before the colon in a different way after the colon.
The department is full of canines (means something similar to) *dogs are in the hall, in the classroom and working in the laboratories.*
In b, the *classic experiment* is explained after the colon.
… classic experiment: a researcher hides food in one of several containers out of sight of the animal – then the chimp is allowed to choose one container after the experimenter indicates the correct choice
In c, the question is explained after the colon.
Those results left researchers with a question: if dogs can pick up on human cues, do they put out cues for humans to understand?

Here is an example of when a colon is used in front of a list. Researchers test a wide variety of animals: chimpanzees, gorillas, wolves, dogs and rats.

2 We can put inverted commas around speech or parts of a text to show that someone else has spoken those words or written that text. (You can also use speech marks " ... ") But, in this context, the writer puts these words ('correct answer') in inverted commas because he is reporting what other people said and he does not agree with them. He does not believe that the answer was really correct.

We can also use inverted commas around metaphors: A modern example is:
Many people have expressed anger over the smoking ban and have said they are now living in a 'nanny-state'.

A nanny is a grandmother. The country is not really being controlled by grandmothers but people feel that the government is treating them like children/behaving like a grandmother.

3 In English, short sentences in formal or academic writing are not appropriate. (although sometimes the writer might use a few short sentences for dramatic purpose) It is therefore better to use a semi-colon when either the preceding or following sentence is fairly short, rather than separating the sentences with a full stop.
the horse didn't actually know arithmetic is too short to be a full academic or formal sentence.

Some writers also use a hyphen (-) instead of a semi-colon.

4 We use commas for many purposes, but in these two examples, they are followed by an explanation of the last subject/noun in the previous clause.
In a, the *study of animal behaviour* is an explanation for *ethology.*
In b, *a breed of dog that herd sheep* is an explanation for *mudi.*

Key for Writing module

Quiz p.46

1 B
2

	How long should you spend on this task?	Minimum number of words
Task 1	20 minutes	150
Task 2	40 minutes	250

3 A, B, D, E
You only have to describe a graph in the Academic test. You may have to present an argument by explaining advantages/disadvantages or explaining 2 opposing views in Task 2 of the General Training Test.

4   C
5   B, C, D, E, G
    It is unlikely that you will be given a question that is easy
    to prepare for and memorize.
    This is why 'describe a historical event in your country'
    and 'describe a famous person' would not appear as a Task
    2 question.
6   A

Skills development p.46

1   C (write a letter of complaint)   B (make an invitation)
    ABC (give factual information)   A (give your opinion
    about a general problem)   AC (make recommendations)
2   Semi-formal/formal = A   Informal = B   Formal = C

Skills practice p.47

Language focus

1
a   concern about
b   anger about
c   gratitude for
d   dissatisfaction with
e   surprise at
f   inform/about
g   to make a complaint to a hotel manager
h   to ask for information about facilities
i   to apologize to a customer

2
a   i
b   ii
c   i
d   i
e   i
f   ii
g   ii

3

a	It's been	ages a while a long time	since	I heard from you. we saw each other. I wrote to you.

b	How are you? How's everything	going?

c	How are you? How are you	getting	on with your	~~family?~~ * new job? training course? studies?

*   A very good friend might ask 'How are you getting on with
    your family?' if he/she knows you often have problems
    with them. Usually someone would just write 'How is your
    family?'

4
a   I hope you feel better soon!   III   A letter offering
                                                        sympathy
b   Give me a call and let me know   IV   A letter suggesting
    what you think.   a plan/idea
c   I hope you sort things out soon.   II   A letter giving
                                                        advice
d   I'm looking forward to meeting   I   A letter
    you.   introducing the
                                                        writer

e   **Give** my love/regards/best wishes to your family.
f   **Have** a great time/weekend/birthday!
g   **Thanks** again for the fantastic present/your help/letting
    me borrow the car.

5
a   I recommend **(that) the council build/builds** more roads in
    this area if we want to reduce traffic jams.
b   Another possibility **is that the council provides** more
    buses.
c   To help the environment, one idea would **be to recycle** our
    paper and glass.
d   If school children **studied** practical subjects, they **would**
    find jobs more easily.
    (It's also possible to say 'study' and 'will find' – but *past
    simple form* and *would + base verb* are more suitable for
    formal suggestions.)
e   In order to be healthy, the first step **is to eat** a balanced diet.
f   I suggest **(that) you provide** more litter bins if you want to
    reduce the amount of litter.
g   Why don't **you try** yoga if you have a bad back?
h   If you want somewhere to stay, how about **staying** with
    me?

6

> To the editor,
> I am writing in response to your recent article on crime.
> In Northbridge there has also been a **considerable** rise in the
> number of burglaries. **In fact,** last week, three houses in the
> street where I live were broken into and **valuable jewellery was
> taken.** The growing amount of vandalism that **can be seen** in the
> town centre is also shocking.
>
> I am certain that this rise is **due to** the fact that
> unemployment is **extremely** high in this area, especially among
> young people. People who have been unemployed for **a long time**
> often become desperate, and young people often feel pressured
> to follow their friends' behaviour, even if it is criminal.
>
> **If the local council offered free training courses for the
> unemployed, it might help them to find jobs** and stay away
> from trouble. Young people need to have self-respect before they
> can respect other people in society.
>
> **I hope something is done** about this situation before too long.
> Yours sincerely
> Jamie Felton

7

Dear Alex,

This is just a short letter to say thank you so much for ~~invite~~ me to your home.
inviting

I ~~had really a~~ great time. I think you live in an incredibly beautiful country!
really had a/had a really

~~Especially~~, I loved our trip in the mountains   , even though I was exhausted!
^especially

On the way home, I had a ten ~~hours~~ wait at Los Angeles airport because of bad
hour

weather. I was really ~~annoying~~ and I spent the rest of my money on lots of cups
annoyed (or It was really annoying)

of coffee. I can't tell you how happy ~~was I~~ to finally get home.
I was

Anyway, I would really like you to come to New York next year. ~~It~~ is plenty of
There

room in my apartment so you could stay here as long ~~time~~ as you like. We could

spend a day wandering round Central Park, see a baseball game — whatever ~~do~~ you

like. It's also worth ~~to spend~~ a whole day at least in the Metropolitan Museum.
spending

Get in touch and let me know what you ~~are thinking~~.
think

Thanks again,
Andy

8 Task 1

Name: Sooyeon Bae

Task Achievement	Coherence and Cohesion	Lexical Resource	Grammatical Range and Accuracy
The student has responded to points 1 + 2 fairly well. She has explained what the problems are (buses are late & the bus drivers sometimes don't have coins for change) and said how they affect people (people are worried about being late for appointments/being late when meeting friends & they always need coins). She has not dealt with point 3. She needed to make suggestions about public transport improvements, but she only asks the manager to make improvements.	The student has used paragraphs well : the first paragraph explains why she is writing, the middle paragraph mentions the particular problems, and the last paragraph explains how people feel. She has used a number of linking words to connect her ideas ie *so, as a result, first, but, second.* Overall, it is easy to understand what the student wants to communicate.	The student's range of vocabulary shows she can express herself in basic situations. She has used some formal vocabulary which helps make the letter sound reasonably polite ie *I would like to talk to you…* *Please would you solve these problems* There are some spelling mistakes with commonly-used words ie *angly* (angry) *affraid* (afraid) *embarssed* (embarrassed) *fortunatly* (fortunately). She has written *annoyed* when she should have written *annoying*. She has used the word *prepare* but she should have said *We always need to have coins for the bus fare.*	The student can use grammar well enough to explain simple ideas but is often not accurate. She often omits possessive pronouns ie (my) *homestay*, (my) *new flat*, (my) *friends* She often omits *s* on plural words ie *some/these problem* *any coins* *to meet friend* There are a number of other errors, sometimes with simple language and sometimes with more complex language, but these do not prevent the reader from understanding.

Probable band: 5

Task Achievement	Coherence and Cohesion	Lexical Resource	Grammatical Range and Accuracy
The student has responded to all three points. She has mentioned the problems (buses are late or leave earlier), she refers to the effects (she has to use her car and leave early/people don't know whether they will be on time for meetings) and she offers some solutions (the buses + bus timetable must be reliable)	The student has used paragraphs well: her ideas and points are sensibly separated which makes it easy for the reader to understand. She has used some linking words effectively ie *because, however, but, so.* Overall, it is easy to understand what the student wants to communicate.	There is evidence that the student has a good range of vocabulary ie *normally, convenient, punctual, set out, insufficient, reliable* The student has made quite a few errors but these do not prevent the reader from understanding ie *the timetable of buses* (the bus timetable), *arrive and departure* (depart), *there are insufficient in car parks* (insufficient spaces in...) *buses' problem* (the bus problem) *pay a parking ticket* (pay for a...) *attent* (attend) *Your sincerely* (Yours)	The student has used a few fairly difficult grammatical structures correctly ie *should be improved, they could not only save time but also money, residents would be happier* The student has often forgotten to use the article *the* ie (the) *town centre* *a rest on* (the) *bus* (the) *timetable* The student has tried to use quite complex conditional/If – sentences but these are inaccurate.

Probable band: 6

Task C A possible model answer:

> *Dear Sir or Madam*
> *I am writing to express my dissatisfaction with the bus service in Edgewater. First of all, there are simply not enough buses for the number of people who need to use them. During morning and evening rush hour, many people find that they cannot board their bus because it is already crowded. This is also true for school children in the afternoon. If people do manage to get on, their journey is extremely uncomfortable.*
>
> *Secondly, the routes that the buses follow do not meet passengers' needs. People who live on River Rd have to walk over a mile to get to the nearest bus stop, and much of the walk is uphill.*
>
> *I strongly suggest that buses should run every ten minutes during peak times and that there are at least two bus stops on River Rd. It would also be extremely helpful if this new bus route took passengers from here to the centre of town, or at least to a connecting bus stop.*
>
> *Thank you for your attention.*
> *Yours faithfully*
> *Mary Mayhew*

Understanding the instructions and the question p.52

1

A False. You can decide how long to spend on each task but it is recommended that you spend 40 minutes on Task 2. You need to plan and write more, and you get more marks for Task 2.

B True.
C False. It is likely that you will need to express your opinion.
D True.
E False. Even when you are expressing your personal view, you should write in a formal way.

2

A give only your personal views? = IV, VII
B show two sides of an argument? = II, VIII
C explain why something has happened? = III, VI
D describe or compare your country to the country in the opening statement? = I, V
E suggest solutions? = III, VI

Understanding the topic and the task p.53

1 B
2 C

Skills practice p.53

1 Main topic: people prefer to have children later on in life
  Task: Do you need to …
  … focus more on the present situation than the past?   YES
  … include the good and bad points about having children when you're older?   YES
  … suggest ways that people with children can be helped by the government?   NO
2 Main topic: people who work in cities suffer from stress
  Task: Do you need to …
  … suggest ways that stress could be reduced?   YES
  … give examples of what might cause people's stress?   YES
  … compare life in the city to life in the countryside?   NO

3 Main topic: traditions and customs in your country –
           changing or staying the same?
  Task: Do you need to …
  … describe some of the customs and traditions in your
     country ?   YES
  … compare your country to Britain?   NO
  … discuss the advantages and disadvantages of keeping
     traditions?   NO

Writing style in Task 2 essays p.54

English native speakers …
1 … write the main purpose of the essay in the **first
    paragraph**
2 … write about different topics in **separate** paragraphs
3 … usually write paragraphs which are **more than two lines**
4 … are usually **direct and assertive** when they make a claim
5 … make a claim and give one or more **factual examples**
6 … **often** mention their own point of view in the opening
    paragraph
7 … normally use **long** sentences in this kind of writing

Brainstorming and planning p.55

1

Beneficial effect	Negative effect
• *informative about national and foreign affairs*	• *encourages laziness/non-activity*
• *helps people experience countries/culture they can't experience directly*	• *poor diet*
• *cheap source of entertainment and information*	• *disappearance of family conversation*
• *can be something whole family enjoy together*	• *TV violence*
• *a 2ⁿᵈ chance at education for some people*	• *a lot of non-educational/stupid programmes*
• *helps people to sympathize/empathize with others*	• *some people desperate to be famous*

4 c

Introduction

- - - - - - - - - - - - - - - -

Main body

- - - - - - - - - - - - - - - -

Conclusion

5 c

The introduction p.56

A This is not a good start because the first two sentences copy
  the question almost exactly. The last sentence is not suitable
  for a formal essay.
B This is a good start because the writer starts with a general
  statement about the effects of television. It is also clear that
  the purpose of the essay is to discuss the influence of
  television.
C This is not a good answer because it is written in a very
  informal style.

The main body pp.56–57

Clearly, television has become the (1) <u>prime source of information for many people</u>.   1
At the touch of a button, we can find out about the **latest economic developments,**   2
changes in social policy, political news and so on. As well as keeping us in touch   3
with current affairs, television offers us an (2) <u>opportunity to experience countries and</u>   4
<u>cultures</u> that we cannot experience directly. This experience is partly responsible   5
for the **change in British food** and our **interest in foreign films and music**.   6
Despite these benefits, there are certainly a number of problems associated with a   7
dependency on television. Firstly, it has been accused of (3) <u>destroying conversation</u>,   8
especially during family meal times. **'How was your day?' has been replaced with**   9
'What's on channel three?'. As it is such a time-consuming passive activity, (4) <u>it can</u>   10
<u>also lead to health problems.</u> Whereas children used to spend a great deal of their   11
free time playing outdoors, they now amuse themselves in front of the TV for hours.   12
This is **bad for their general fitness, eyesight and ability to concentrate** on more   13
active interests.

Linking words p.57

1
clearly / it is obvious that / there is no doubt that
as well as   not only does   in addition to
is responsible for / has led to / has resulted in
despite / however / on the other hand
associated with / related to / connected to
especially / in particular / mainly
as / since / because
whereas / in comparison to / while

2
a There is no doubt that the effects of pollution have become
  widespread.
b People, teenagers in particular, often feel under pressure to
  behave like others in their group.
  (or)
  People often feel under pressure to behave like others in
  their group, teenagers in particular.
c In comparison to the past, it is now common to take (a
  foreign holiday / a holiday abroad).
d The huge amount of fat and sugar in our food has led to the
  modern problem of obesity.
e In addition to encouraging people to buy goods they don't
  need, advertisements often make people feel dissatisfied
  with their lives.
f Global tourism has provided many people with
  employment. However, it has (also) often destroyed their
  environment (too).
g A high crime rate is often related to high unemployment.

h   Not only do we need to offer free languages courses to recent immigrants, we (also) need to help them overcome their culture shock (too).
i   The internet and email have resulted in more people working from home.

Conclusion pp.57–58

1

A   This conclusion is the most suitable: it states the writer's own opinion and avoids repeating all the points made before.
B   This is not suitable; it is too brief and too informal.
C   This is not suitable because it simply repeats the points that were already made.

2

(a) **In conclusion/To sum up**, it is probably
(b) **fair to say/true** that the benefits of television
(c) **outweigh/outnumber** its negative effects. What we need to do now is to
(d) **ensure/make sure** that television keeps its promise to educate and entertain,
(e) **so that we can/in order to** improve our lives and not limit them.

Claims and supporting sentences p.58

	Claim	Supporting sentence or example
Introduction *example*	*more people having children in their thirties/forties*	*not necessary – the claim is made in the task*
Paragraph 2	*Older people more financially secure*	*Provide a house/have savings + income*
	Raising children requires patience + flexibility	*Parents lose sleep/must give up a lot of their free time*
Paragraph 3	*raising children is physically demanding*	*Parents tired when children want to play*
	big generation gap	*Parents + teenagers don't understand each other*
	elderly grandparents	*Little interaction/little support*
Conclusion	*Impossible to generalize about best time to have children*	*Depends on parents*
		Important thing is love/being looked after

Linking words p.59

Addition	Contrast	Cause	Consequence
1 furthermore	1 Having said that	1 For this reason,	1 therefore
2 as well as this			2 (this/it) may mean that

Useful words and phrases p.59

a it is (also) true that …
b one reason for …
c it may be the case …
d to generalize (about something) …

Punctuation p.59

It is certainly true that, until recently, most couples got married and had children in   1
their early or mid twenties, sometimes even earlier. However, there is now a   2
definite trend towards having children in your thirties, even early forties. How will   3
this development effect the family?   4
One reason for starting a family later is that the parents are usually more financially secure
than younger couples; this means that they can provide a decent house and   5
have a regular job or savings to support their children. Furthermore, new parents   6
will lose a lot of sleep and will have to give up much of their free time to look after
their baby's needs. Raising young children, therefore, requires patience and   7
flexibility. Older couples may have acquired these skills through their greater life experience.
Having said that, taking care of a child is a physically-demanding task. It may be   8
the case that older parents become tired when their child still wants to play. As well
as this, the greater generation gap may mean that parents and their teenagers have   9
little in common. For this reason, they may find it difficult to communicate and   10
understand each other's way of thinking. Unfortunately, it is also true that the   11
children's grandparents may be elderly and unable to have much interaction with
them. Nowadays, it is common to hear parents complain that they have no support   12
from family.
In conclusion, we cannot really generalize about the best time to have a child. It   13
depends on the personality and personal circumstances of each potential mother or
father. The most important thing is simply that the child is loved and looked after.

Comments on students' sample answers

Task 2

Name: Marwan Salem Saeed Al Khatri (p.60)

Task Response	Coherence and Cohesion	Lexical Resource	Grammatical Range and Accuracy
The student has understood the task: he mentions the causes of stress (crowds & too many cars) and makes some suggestions. However, because the student does not have enough language or cannot use language correctly, it is not always possible to understand exactly what the suggestions are ie *The government should get tax for drivers who parking his car/ the government should charge for who have car.* The suggestions about installing more traffic lights and having more public transport are easier to understand.	The student has used paragraphs to separate his ideas. However, it is difficult for the reader to understand the student's argument. The student does not use linking words well so we cannot always understand the connection between ideas. He often forgets to put a full stop between sentences so we cannot always see where a new sentence/new idea begins.	The student's range of vocabulary shows he can talk about simple, everyday topics. There is evidence of some good vocabulary eg *install traffic lights* *emergency call* *to become busy* However, he is often inaccurate and this limits his ability to communicate clearly eg *the head of noisy* (the main cause of noise?) *the horn motorbikes* (the horns of motorbikes?) *to impose people to change to taxi* (to force people to change to taxis?) There are some basic spelling mistakes eg buecause (because) ues (use)	The student's main weakness is his lack of grammatical range and accuracy. There are many basic mistakes, often with simple language eg plural forms eg *this cities has problem* (these cities have problems) *more traffic light* (traffic lights) Other basic problems include *all people they want .* (Everyone wants ...) *drivers who want to parking his cars* (driver who want to park their cars) *the lessest cities crowd or noisy in the world* (the least crowded and noisy city in the world)

Probable band: 4

Name: Amy Mun Yin Wu (p.61)

Task Response	Coherence and Cohesion	Lexical Resource	Grammatical Range and Accuracy
The student has clearly understood the task: she mentions the causes of stress (traffic jams/crowds of people) and makes some suggestions (people should be persuaded to use public transport/road tax should be increased/some businesses and industries should be moved outside the city)	The student has used paragraphs to organize her points: there is a general introduction, the next paragraph deals with the first cause of stress, the next with the second cause, the fourth paragraph offers solutions, and there is a general summary. She has some used basic linking words to connect/introduce ideas ie *but, so, firstly, secondly* It is easy for the reader to follow the student's argument.	There is evidence of a good range of vocabulary, ie *undoubtedly, drawbacks, tend, serious traffic problem, destination, green organization, persuade* The student sometimes makes errors with word formation but these do not prevent the reader from understanding ie *the economy development* (economic development) *have the patient* (the patience)	The student has a limited range of grammatical structures. She is generally accurate when she uses the present simple form, but there are a number of errors with other structures eg *More and more big cities are appeared* (...cities are appearing) *that make you cannot do what you want* (that means you cannot do what you want) *that makes the stress staying in your mind* (that makes the stress worse/that means you feel stressed) She has used *can* incorrectly or unnaturally in the fourth paragraph: eg *Some green organizations can* (could/should) *persuade people to use more public transport, and the government can* (could/should) *increase road tax. That can* (would) *make people use public transport, so the traffic can* (would) *be reduced.*

Probable band: 5

Language work p.61

1 1 however
   2 so
   3 moreover
   4 and for this reason
   5 because
   6 but
   7 this
   8 these
   9 regarding
  10 this
  11 which

p.62

2 a True. They are both used to refer to or introduce a subject or topic.

   b True

   c False. You can only use *which* when you want to add extra information. For example, in the essay :
Secondly, the government could transfer some businesses and industries outside
the city = the necessary information
which would reduce the population in some of the more populated places. = extra information. (Look in your grammar books for relative clauses if you want to know more about this.)

   d True, they have the same meaning, but in good formal writing, *but* and *however* are used like this:
People can earn a good salary if they work in the city <u>but</u> they often feel stressed and tired.
People can earn a good salary if they work in the city.
<u>However,</u> they often feel stressed and tired.

   e False. When *so* is followed by a result or a consequence, it should connect two clauses. It should not start a sentence e.g.
People tend to use their private cars <u>so</u> this causes a traffic jam.

Key for Speaking module

Quiz p.63

1 B

2 1 True
   2 False. This is not an IELTS task.
   3 True
   4 True
   5 False. You have to speak for 1–2 minutes.
   6 False. You are given a card with a topic and some prompts to help you.
   7 True
   8 True
   9 False. This is the most challenging part of the module as you are asked to talk about more abstract issues and ideas.

Talking about familiar topics p.63

Possible questions:

Your studies
How long have you been studying English?
Why is it important for you to learn English?
Who was your favourite teacher at school? Why did you like their lessons?
What are you planning to study?
Why are you taking IELTS ?

Your previous work experience (if any), your current job or your future career plans
What do you do? (Be careful with this question. It means *What is your job?*)
What are/were the best things about your job?
What are your ambitions?

Your family/home life
Tell me about your family.
What does your father do? (or mother)
Do you live with your family?
Do you have a large family?
How long have you been here?
Tell me about where you are living at the moment.

Your country
How would you describe your home country/home town?
What are the best things about life in your country?
How is life in your country different from life here?

Your hobbies and interests
What are your main hobbies?
Do you enjoy travelling?
What do you usually do at the weekend?
Are you interested in playing sport?
What type of music/films do you enjoy most?

Giving a good answer p.63

2 A Not enough information. A good example would be: *Mr Wallis, our chemistry teacher. He made the subject really interesting, and although he was very strict, he was also quite funny.*

B Doesn't answer the question. Be careful of learning phrases by heart and then just using them even when they're not appropriate. A good example would be: *I started learning English at school when I was only 10, but the lessons weren't very good. I've been studying properly for about three years, though.*

C A good answer. This answers the question and adds a little extra information as well. It also sounds fluent and is accurate.

D A good answer. Again, this answers the question and gives a little extra information. The beginning, *Oh definitely … sounds very natural.*

E Not enough information. Don't make the mistake of thinking that the less you say, the fewer mistakes you will make! The examiner needs to be able to assess your fluency and you are expected to give more than one-word answers. A good example would be: *No, I don't. I live with three other students in a shared house. It's quite close to college, so it's convenient.*

F Doesn't answer the question. Be careful with *How long* + present perfect. Remember this refers to past time up to now. A good example would be: *I came in April, so I suppose I've been here about six months now.*

G Not fluent enough. It's good to show you have a wide vocabulary, but it's more important to communicate fluently. A good example would be: *It's a small house near to the town centre. It's not very attractive, but it's comfortable and the rent's quite cheap.*

H A good answer. This answers the question, gives some extra information and is correct and fluent.

Identifying strengths and weaknesses p.64

Although the student's answers are not monosyllabic, many of the responses are rather brief and could be more fully developed (*Five years. I studied at high school in China*). There are a few grammatical inaccuracies (*I usually do play ping pong, the product major is charcoal*) and a rather limited range of vocabulary but some evidence of wider lexical knowledge (*managing director, fitness clubs*). Some inappropriate use of vocabulary (*charcoal town*). Pronunciation is generally good, but the intonation is heavily influenced by her native language and would benefit from flowing more freely. There aren't many words or phrases to make her responses sound more natural or to gain more time and there are quite a few hesitations.

Overall, the student would need to focus on improving fluency and producing more extended responses as well as aiming to show a wider, more accurate use of language.

Planning your answer p.65

1 and **2**

Describe <u>an occasion</u> when <u>you</u> have been <u>successful</u>.
You need to talk about one occasion or event in your life (any time up to the present) when you were successful.
- where and when you were successful – give the background (school, home, college, work, how old you were)

- how you were successful – *say what happened (won a race/passed an exam)*
- what you had to do – *give examples: studied hard/worked hard/prepared in some way/asked for help*
- how you felt – *very happy because/very excited because …*

Giving extra information p.65

Talk about <u>an important day</u> in <u>your life.</u>
- when this day was – *the day my football team got promoted*
- if you were alone or with others – *with my brother and others in crowd*
- where you were/what happened – *got to football ground, waited for game to start, lots of people, final goals – we won!*
- and explain why this day was important to you – *first time team had ever been promoted*

Sample answer:
OK, the important day in my life that I'm going to talk about happened about four years ago. This was the day my football team got promoted. The team, er, had played well all that season and had reached the finals, and my brother and I were, er, were both keen supporters and we both followed the team, er, for about fifteen years. It was a very exciting day for, for the team because they'd never been promoted to, er, out of the division into a higher division in their history.

My brother and I got to the football ground about lunchtime and waited for the game to start as the crowd built up- there were about 10,000 people there that day. The game swung from side to side, with, first of all, our team scoring and then the opposing team scoring twice, which was why it was fantastic when our team scored two goals in the last five minutes to win the day and gain promotion to the higher division. The noise at the final whistle was amazing and we were all incredibly excited. I don't think I've ever been to a game where there was such a great atmosphere, before or since. We really celebrated that night, but the next morning, I could hardly speak from all of the shouting I'd been doing!

The speaker has included the key points, then added extra details to make the talk more interesting.

Identifying strengths and weaknesses p.66

Student 1
This answer is quite short and does not satisfactorily cover all the points on the card. However, it has quite a good range of language and is quite accurate.

Student 2
Level of communicative ability is high. Some hesitations but clear that the speaker has a very natural style and produces a measured, thoughtful response to the points on the card.

Follow-up questions p.66

1 1D   2E   3C   4F   5B   6A

Expanding answers p.66

1   *Possible answers*
Yes, I think it's a good idea – especially as you get older <u>because</u> it can help to keep your body active. It's important to make time for exercise, even when you're busy, <u>so</u> I try to go to the gym three times a week. If I'm honest, <u>however,</u> it's usually more like twice a week.

2 Well, no, I don't think there is really. It probably just seems that way because it's reported in all the newspapers <u>and</u> on the television. I think there has always been quite a lot of crime in big cities, <u>although</u> there may be more crime <u>such as</u> house-breaking in rural communities these days.

3 Well, it's certainly useful to have one. <u>On the other hand</u> I find it really annoying when I'm on the train and everyone's talking into their mobile phones. I think there should be more control about when and where people can use them.

Linking ideas p.67

1 1 because
2 so
3 and
4 however, on the other hand
5 such as

Model answers:
1 Do you think smoking will be banned in all public places?
I hope it will! I hate going into smoky pubs and restaurants. However, I don't think it's very likely to happen here for a while even though it's already happened in some countries.

2 Do you prefer to go out or stay at home in the evening?
I prefer going out. It's so boring just staying at home and watching TV. However, I can't always afford to go out when I want to.

3 Do you think that email has made our lives easier?
It's amazing being able to keep in touch with my friends and family so easily, but I can't help thinking that email has actually created more work for most people. I often get 40–50 messages a day – far more than I ever got on paper or by phone.

4 Which is better: living in the countryside or in the city?
Well, on the one hand, it's certainly cleaner and quieter in the countryside, but I think I would miss the nightlife if I lived there – it could be a bit too quiet! I might move to the countryside when I'm a bit older.

5 Are qualifications important?
Yes, definitely. I strongly believe that you must have good qualifications these days if you want to get a good job. Maybe it was different in the past, but nowadays employers expect more.

6 How likely is it that computers will be able to do your job in the future?
I doubt very much if computers could take over the job of a nurse. OK, they could do some of the monitoring of patients, but they'd never be able to give the support we do.

7 Would you rather watch sport or play it?
Well, it probably depends on the sport. I'd rather watch boxing than actually do it. It's not as dangerous! But I like playing and watching football. I particularly like going to see live matches.

8 What do you think the consequences of global warming will be?
It's bound to have more and more of an effect on the weather. I think there's a good chance that the climate of Britain will change quite noticeably over the next few years, which could cause all sorts of problems.

Key for Practice test

Listening
1 C
2 B
3 Moseley
4 third (floor)
5 No
6 £520
7 B
8 375 Greenfield Rd/Road (NOT Green Field)
9 357629
10 4.15
11 two or three/2–3
12 up the coast/north
13 the sun
14 hat/cap
15 well-known/obvious
16 (to) towards the shore (beach)/against the rip
17 across the current/parallel to shore
18 lessens/reduces/gets weaker
19 swim alone
20 a lifeguard
21 Biology
22 cotton
23 expense/they're expensive/cost
24 eat harmful bugs (insects)/pollinate crops
25/26/27 A, C and D in any order
28 painted/applied
29 flowers
30 wings
31 partnership
32 (a) person/human being
33 one person
34 every year/yearly/once a year
35 make (the) (important) decisions
36 capital/money/investment
37 shares (of stock)
38 employees/workers
39 profit/money
40 B

Reading
1 accommodation
2 tourist facilities
3 July and August
4 public transport
5 12 months
6 guided tour
7 campsite
8 hire a sheet
9 B
10 F
11 F
12 E
13 C
14 D
15 F
16 NG
17 F
18 NG
19 T
20 T
21 T

22 nationality
23 progress
24 two/2 week
25 expertise
26 five/5 hours
27 assessment
28 A
29 C
30 B
31 D
32 A
33 E
34 H
35 F
36 B
37 C
38 H
39 B
40 D

Writing

Model answer for Task 1:

> To the editor,
>
> I am writing in the hope that one of your readers can help me. Last Thursday afternoon I took a walk along Cheltenham Beach. There was hardly anyone else there except a mother and her two young children, and an old man and his dog. As I walked along the beach the dog ran and jumped up at me. It was friendly and wanted to play but it knocked me over and I think that this was when I lost my bracelet.
>
> This bracelet is not particularly expensive but it has a lot of sentimental value. It was given to me by my mother and I have had it for twenty three years. As you can imagine, I would really like to get it back.
>
> It is a plain, silver bracelet with a red stone in the centre. My name is engraved on the inside. If someone has found my bracelet, I would be very grateful if they could return it to me at the above address.
>
> Yours faithfully
>
> Melissa Stokes   (Word count 171)

Model answer for Task 2:

> It is not simple to define poverty: for some people 'being poor' means not being able to afford the consumer items that make life more comfortable, whereas for others, it means not being able to eat. What is easier to see is that the gap between the rich and poor is growing.
>
> First of all, many people believe that the government should deal with this problem. It should make sure that every child is properly fed and clothed and has a good standard of education. Although it may cost a great deal of money to do this, it may prevent another generation growing up with no opportunities and no hope for the future. Furthermore, the governments of wealthier countries should also give financial assistance to the people of poorer countries: there should be no reason why some people are dying from starvation or easily treatable illnesses in the 21st century.
>
> On the other hand, some people feel that poor people have caused many of their own problems. They often give the example of poor people having too many children and refusing to find work to support their family. They believe that many poor people are lazy and depend on the government to hand out large sums of money. However, it is hard to support this argument when you see people suffering from malnutrition and disease in some third-world countries.
>
> In conclusion, we need a solution that helps poorer people to become self-sufficient. If you just hand out money, the money will run out. If you can provide education and training, this can last forever.
>
> (Word count 264)

Recording scripts

Recording 01

[K = Keiko, S = Stephen]

K: Um, excuse me. Do you know where the accommodation office is?

S: Yes, of course. Are you a new student?

K: Yeah. I only arrived here yesterday, so I still feel a bit lost.

S: I've only been here a couple of weeks, but it doesn't take long to find your way around. The campus isn't that big. The accommodation office is in the main building.

K: Is that the three storey building by the lake?

S: No – look, it's that big building there behind the trees. The one with the glass front. Go in through the main door – then up the steps.

K: You mean the door on the right-hand side?

S: Yeah. Then, when you get inside, go straight down the corridor, to the far end, and turn left. You'll see three doors on your left – accommodation is the middle one.

K: So, I go along the corridor, turn left, and it's the second door on the left?

S: That's right!

K: Thanks very much for your help.

S: No problem, see you around. My name is Stephen, by the way.

K: Oh, OK, great. I'm Keiko.

Recording 02

[K = Keiko, AO = Accommodation Officer]

K: Excuse me, am I in the right place to look for accommodation?

AO: Are you a student here?

K: Yes, I just arrived yesterday, and I was looking for some help with finding a place to live.

AO: Well, you've come to the right place! What sort of accommodation are you looking for?

K: I'm not sure really. Could you tell me what's available?

AO: Of course. There are three kinds of accommodation that we deal with – home stays, college halls of residence, or private lets.

K: Home stays? Is that where you live with a family?

AO: Yes, that's right. Usually you have your own room, and maybe your own bathroom, but you live with a local family and they provide you with meals, access to a washing machine, all of that kind of thing. That's $130 per week, or $90 without meals.

K: Yes, I did think about doing that. It would be a good way to practise my English, but I think I'd really prefer to live with people more my own age, other students, for example.

AO: Of course. Well, the college has a small residential block, with rooms for 50 students, but it's very popular and I think at the moment it's full.

K: That's a shame.

AO: Yes, students like it. You have your own study bedroom, with a bed, a table, chair and a washbasin, and then you share a bathroom and kitchen with four other students.

K: It sounds nice. Never mind. What was the other option that you mentioned?

AO: The other one is, um, private lets. These are flats and houses owned by private landlords, not the college, but we make sure that you are paying a reasonable price so it's a bit easier than just looking in the newspaper to find a flat.

K: That sounds good. Would it be for one person or more?

AO: It depends. Mostly, flats are for three to four students, but there are sometimes one bedroom flats available.

Recording 03

[K = Keiko, AO = Accommodation Officer]

K: So, how can I find out about the flats or rooms that are available at the moment?

AO: Well, I can give you all of that, but if you wouldn't mind, first of all, I'll take down a few contact details and then if something suitable comes up, I'll be able to tell you.

K: OK, great.

AO: So, what's your name, please?

K: Keiko Jenkins.

AO: Sorry, could you spell that for me, please?

K: Of course. It's K-E-I-K-O and my surname is J-E-N-K-I-N-S.

AO: Thank you. What's your nationality? I thought that you must be Japanese, but Jenkins is an English name.

K: Yes, it is. My father is English, and I have British nationality, but I grew up in Japan, so I feel more Japanese.

AO: How interesting. So, Keiko, where are you staying at the moment?

K: At the Sunrise Guest House. It's number 562 Green Park Road.

AO: 562 Green Park Road. Fine. And do you have a contact number?

K: I've got a mobile. It's 07785 265 981.

AO: Sorry, I didn't quite get that. Was it 256 891?

K: No, 07785 265 981.

AO: Thanks. And email? Have you got an address you can access easily?

K: Yeah, it's keiko@hotmail.com

AO: That's fine. OK …

Recording 04

15
50
162
£3.25
47%
0.54
12,651

Recording 05

U Y J O G X I P Z W H A Q R E B

Recording 06

1 forward slash
2 hyphen
3 colon
4 semi-colon
5 dot

Recording 07

1 A: Sorry. What was that name again – Sir Anthony …?
   B: Sir Anthony Winton, that's A-N-T-H-O-N-Y.　W-I-N-T-O-N.
2 A: So what's the answer, then?
   B: 34.92.
3 A: Could I just take your address?
   B: Certainly, it's 15 Sparrow Lane. Sparrow is S-P-A double-R-O-W.
4 A: How high is Everest?
   B: Let me look it up. Mm, it says here 29,030 feet.
5 A: What's his name again?
   B: Michael MacWilliams – M-I-C-H-A-E-L . M-A-C-W-I double-L-I-A-M-S.
6 A: … and I live at 286 Banbury Road.
   B: How do you spell Banbury?
   A: B-A-N-B-U-R-Y.
   B: Thanks.
7 A: So, what did I get in the test?
   B: 74%.
   A: Great!
8 A: Who's your favourite author?
   B: Mm, that's hard, but I think it must be Janet Gates.
9 A: So what was the number again?
   B: 0121 674 95 double 4.
10 A: Do you have a reference number on that letter?
   B: Um, yes, I think so. Here it is … reference number 654/120084.
11 A: OK, is it Mrs J Smith?
   B: No. Mrs J Robson-Smith.
12 A: … and what's your address there?
   B: Flat 3, 547 Oxford Road.
13 A: What was the web address of that company?
   B: I think it was www. bht.co.uk
14 A: Could I make an appointment, please?
   B: Which doctor do you usually see?
   A: Dr. Brown.
15 A: What's the registration of the car?
   B: N 770 CES.

Recording 08

[D = Dan, RM = Restaurant Manager]

RM: Hello, Giovanni's Italian Restaurant. Can I help you?
   D: Hello, yes, I hope so. I'm phoning to enquire about booking a party at your restaurant. Do you cater for large groups?
RM: Yes, we do, but the maximum we can seat together is 24.
   D: Oh, that's fine. I think there'll be about 18 of us.
RM: Fine, no problem. We have a large room at the back of the restaurant that we usually use for groups. It means that you are not disturbed by the other customers.
   D: That sounds fantastic. Does it cost extra for that?

RM: No, no, no, we just ask that you spend at least £10 per person on your meal.
   D: That seems reasonable. Is it one long table?
RM: No, it's three round tables. Each table will seat eight people. We find that's a bit more of a friendly way of eating – you can talk to more people, and there's more space on the table for the food!
   D: Oh, yes – that's important!
RM: So when do you want to come?
   D: Well, we'd like a Friday or Saturday night really, maybe April the 15th?
RM: Let me see. Oh, I'm sorry, the 15th is already fully booked. I have a space on the 16th – that's the Saturday. Is that any good?
   D: It's not really what we wanted, but it'll be OK.
RM: Or the week before? I have a space on Friday the 8th.
   D: That's a bit early, really. No, the 16th will be fine.
RM: Usually when we have larger groups we do a set menu – three courses and coffee for a fixed price. Is that what you were looking for?
   D: Is there any choice about the different courses?
RM: But of course! We don't expect everyone to want exactly the same thing! For each course there is a choice of three different dishes, it may be a prawn cocktail to start with for example, or a soup, or maybe a plate of Italian ham and cold meat – we call it *antipasto*.
   D: Great. Just one other thing … I know that a few people in the group are vegetarian. Do you do a vegetarian option?
RM: Absolutely. At least one of the choices for each course is made without meat or fish.
   D: That all sounds great. Is coffee included in the price, did you say?
RM: Certainly … cappuccino, espresso whatever you like.
   D: OK. So how much do you usually charge for the set menu?
RM: For parties of under ten people, it's £15 a head. If you have more than ten it's a bit cheaper!
   D: As I said, I think it'll be about 18 people.
RM: In that case, we can do it for £12 a head. That doesn't include wine or drinks, of course.
   D: No, I understand. Well, that all sounds very good.
RM: There is only one other thing – for larger groups like this, we like to take a deposit a week before you are planning to come – 10% would be fine.
   D: Oh, OK. 10% – that'd be 10% of £12 multiplied by 18 people … how much is that?
RM: Wait, I have a calculator here … um … it's £21.60. Call it £25 to make it a round number.
   D: OK, so I need to give you £25 a week before the 16th of April?
RM: Perfect!
   D: Right, well, I'll finalize the numbers and get back to you in the next couple of weeks to give you the deposit.
RM: Lovely. We look forward to your visit, Mr …
   D: Glover, Dan Glover.
RM: Sorry, can you spell that, Mr Glover?
   D: Sure, it's G-L-O-V-E-R.
RM: Thank you. And could I take a contact telephone number for you?
   D: Of course. My work number is probably best – it's 01452 863092.
RM: Thank you very much. We look forward to seeing you.
   D: Goodbye.

Recording 09

Hello again, and welcome to *You can do it*, the programme that aims to help give you inside information into life's trickier tasks. Today we're going to talk about the different ways there are of buying a used car, something that very few people feel confident about. And let's face it, a mistake can be expensive, as well as very inconvenient.

So your old car has broken down again, and you're feeling that this really is the end for it and it's not worth repairing, or maybe you've just passed your test and are desperate to get out on the road. You look at new cars, but they are so expensive – what can you do? Well, there are three main places to look for a used car, and they all have their advantages and their disadvantages. The first place, and probably the one that most people would go to first, is a used car dealer. These are showrooms where you can go and choose from a range of second-hand cars. Obviously some places are bigger than others, and some are better than others. On the whole, this kind of place is probably the safest way of buying a car as you'll get some kind of warranty. Typically this is about three to six months, maybe a year on a newer car, so if something goes wrong with the car after you've bought it you can take it back – you've got some kind of guarantee. The problem, of course, is that you'll pay for it. Cars from dealers are usually about 800 to £1,000 more expensive than the same type of car bought privately. Quite often dealers will offer you a discount, especially if you've got an old car to trade in, and that might make it seem very attractive. Many will offer you credit, too, so that you don't have to pay for the car straightaway, but it's always good to remember that although this is an expensive way to buy a car, it's probably the safest.

Recording 10

If you're looking for a cheaper car, one way to go about it is to buy a car privately – usually by looking in the adverts in your local paper. This can be a really good way of buying a car, but takes quite a bit more effort. You have to get the paper each week, look through all of the adverts to see if there is anything suitable, make phone calls to arrange a time to see the car, and then travel to view it. The obvious problem is that once you've bought the car it's yours and you can't really take it back. It's probably a really good idea, if you know nothing about cars, to get a mechanic to check it over for you before you buy it.

The final place that you can buy cars is at auction. There are auction rooms up and down the country where cars are sold to whoever will pay the highest price for them. This is definitely the cheapest way of buying a car, but it's also the most risky because you won't really have time to check the car over. So unless you're a mechanic, or don't mind taking a risk, this probably isn't the best way of buying a car. You can find some real bargains, though!

Well, we're now going over to our reporters who have been trying out these different methods, let's hear what they think …

Recording 11

Good morning, everyone. It's good of you all to come, especially those of you who have come straight from sports coaching. For those of you who don't know me, my name is Jenny Arnold and I'm the university Health and Fitness Officer. Today we've got another in our occasional health lectures. This time, with the summer drawing closer and many of you off on holiday, I wanted to talk a bit about being safe and keeping healthy while you're travelling.

Actually, the time to start thinking about this is a few weeks before you go away. If you're going to a foreign country, it's a really good idea to check out any vaccinations that you need. Your GP can tell you this, or you can call up NHS Direct, the free medical telephone service and talk to one of the nurses there. Don't leave it until the last minute, because for some of the vaccinations you'll have to have two shots with a week or two between them. Your local doctor, as well as giving you advice, can give you most of these injections and they should be free as you are students, but you may have to pay for things like malaria tablets if you are going to a country where malaria is a problem.

The other thing that you should arrange before you leave is travel insurance. You might think that this is a waste of money, and it can be quite expensive if you are going somewhere exotic, or doing dangerous sports or activities such as diving or skiing. But it does mean that you can relax and enjoy your holiday, knowing that if anything terrible did happen to you, then you'd be covered financially, at least, and could get home safely.

While you are away, especially if you are going somewhere hot, as many of you probably want to then do take care in the sun. Most of us, here in the UK, don't see much sunshine for most of the year, and if you suddenly expose your skin to the midday sun, without any sun cream, you'll just end up looking very red and feeling very sore. It's not a good start to your holiday and there can be dangerous long-term consequences from skin cancer, too.

Finally, take a few sensible precautions about eating and drinking to avoid illness. Be careful about drinking the water if you are visiting less developed countries and remember that this includes things like cleaning your teeth and ice in your drinks. It's always fun to try new food when you are away, but you might find that you have a slightly upset stomach for the first couple of days, just while you get used to it. Make sure that you keep drinking plenty of liquid – bottled water is best, but soft drinks and fruit juice are OK in moderation too. Take a couple of tablets for it if it gets very bad. You can get these from any chemist here.

Well, I hope that that's been helpful. If you have any other questions, I'm in room 5B, just pop in and ask me.

Recording 12

[R = Robert, A = Anand, C = Claire]

R: Hi there, Anand. What are you up to?

A: Hi Robert. Hi Claire. I'm just having a look at the group project that we've got to do this term.

C: The ecology one?

A: Mm, that's the one.

R: Well, we've probably caught you at a good time then. Claire and I were hoping we could have a bit of a chat about it with you. We're doing it together, aren't we? Have you got a minute now, or are you busy?

A: No, it's OK. Now is a good time. We do need to think about starting work on it, don't we?

C: The main question seems to be knowing where to start. I know that we have to identify an environmental problem somewhere in the world and look at what kind of measures have been taken to limit it, but it's difficult to narrow it down to one!

Recording 13

[R = Robert, A = Anand, C = Claire]

A: Yeah, trying to think of a topic is a problem, isn't it? I've been thinking about it, but it was only the major disasters that I could think of – you know the recent ones that have been in the news.

R: Like what?

A: Oh, you know, water pollution like the oil tanker that broke up and killed all the sea life for miles near Spain, or the kind of thing that's always talked about, like global warming.

C: Do you think we should choose something like that?

A: No! Oh, it'd be such a major piece of work if we did.

R: What's the word limit again? Is it 1,500 words, as usual?

A: No, this one's 500 words longer.

C: 2,000? Help! We've got more work than I thought!

A: Have you got any ideas for a topic?

R: One or two. I was having trouble, too, I looked through books in the library and some journals, but what worked in the end was an Internet search.

A: What did you search for?

R: I put in *environmental* and *disaster* and then did some other searches using words like *sea*, or *river* or *soil erosion*.

A: And that helped?

R: Well, sort of! It gave me a lot of information. My first search came up with 372,000 sites! Obviously I didn't look through them all, but browsing through some gave me an idea for the assignment. How about looking at the problems of pollution in Sydney Harbour?

Recording 14

[R = Robert, A = Anand, C = Claire]

C: The harbour? It'd be local, but it looks pretty clean to me!

R: It is now, but it used to be a real problem. Sewage, for example, used to be emptied directly into the harbour.

A: Yuck! Imagine swimming in all of that waste water. It's not a nice thought, is it?

C: You said it *used to be* a problem …

R: Yes. Sewage is taken out in pipes a long way out to sea now. The City Council constructed them in the 1970s. Unless there is very bad weather, it's solved the problem.

C: What other problems are there?

R: Well, of course there is a fair bit of pollution from the traffic on the harbour.

C: You mean all of the boats?

R: Yes. There are the ferries, of course, but also the commercial and trading vessels. It's still an issue. The State government has set targets for reduction in emissions by next year, they can't stop boats using the harbour, can they?

A: I guess one of the other problems must just be people dumping rubbish – bottles, plastic bags, stuff that people can't be bothered to dispose of properly.

R: Yeah, that's right. There's quite a good story behind that one, though. It's an ongoing project – it's not finished yet, but a lot of it has been removed.

C: How did they manage that? It must be a really difficult job.

R: Local diving clubs who like to dive in the Harbour go down and pick up old bottles and things like that off the bottom of the sea. I think they have a special day once a year to do it.

Recording 15

[R = Robert, A = Anand, C = Claire]

A: So, do you think those are the three main areas we should look at for our assignment?

R: Well, that seems to make sense to me, at least it's reasonably limited.

C: I think we should make some notes, so that we can divide up the work.

A: Yeah, that's a good idea. So, tell us again, what do the divers do?

R: It's in their interests, really – they want to dive in clean water, so they go down and pick up old bottles and cans, things like that. I think that they leave the rubbish if any marine life has started living in it – they wouldn't want to make a crab homeless!

C: That's great, isn't it?

A: So the Harbour is really clean, now?

R: Well, not bad. When the weather is bad, especially if there's a lot of rain and a wind blowing towards the shore, the sewage can still be blown in to the beaches.

C: Not very nice … but I suppose it's not very often. I heard that people using jet skis and small motor boats was a problem.

R: Yeah, I read about that, too. Emissions are actually getting worse, despite what the government wants to happen.

C: You would think that that kind of thing would make people who live here really angry.

R: You would, but actually, they get much more bothered when they have to swim in waste water, after a storm …

Recording 16

1 The college is on the site of an old castle.
2 The meeting will be held on the sixth of February.
3 Please hand your essays in by next Wednesday.
4 We suggest that you take the test in May.
5 The course is inexpensive and highly beneficial.
6 Unemployment rose dramatically in 2001.
7 I would advise you to do your homework.
8 He was a very successful politician.
9 Different companies have different management systems.
10 He had a very successful career.
11 Studying abroad can help you become more independent.
12 Receiving unwanted emails, or *spam*, is a growing problem.

Recording 17

[B = Brenda, C = Cathy]

B: Hi Cathy, I haven't seen you around for ages. Where have you been?

C: Oh, I've been here, but I've been studying really hard, and not going out much, so that's probably why I haven't seen you. I seem to spend all of my time in the library, or in my room with my nose in a book!

B: So your course is hard work?

C: Yes, it is, but it's mainly because we're coming to the end of the year and I've got a few major assignments to get in.

B: Actually, I wanted to talk to you about your course. You're on the Foundation Programme, aren't you?

C: Yeah, that's right. Are you thinking of doing it next year?

B: Maybe. I want to study at a British university, but I'm not sure whether it would be better to do 'A' levels, or a Foundation Course. Which do you think would be better?

C: Well, the big advantage of a Foundation Course is that it only takes a year – 'A' levels take two.

B: Really? That's a big difference!

C: Mm, it is. With 'A' levels, you usually study two or three subjects, and you may not get any extra language support. With a Foundation, you study five or six modules, but they are all connected to one subject – usually the one you want to study at university, for example Business, or IT, and you do extra English classes, too – mostly about six hours a week.

B: That sounds helpful.

C: And another good thing about it is that you don't have to take any exams on the Foundation – well, not any major ones, anyway. All of the marks come from continuous assessment, you know, from your assignments and presentations, that kind of thing. 'A' levels have some continuous assessment, but a lot of your marks come from the final exam.

B: That's a bit scary … So, if the Foundation is so much shorter and has no exams, why would anyone want to do 'A' levels?

C: Good question. I didn't want to and Foundation Courses tend to be popular with students from overseas, but I think most British students do 'A' levels. It's part of their education system. Also, to be honest, if you get good 'A' levels, it gives you a lot more choice about which university you can go to. All British universities recognize 'A' levels, but some don't recognize Foundation Courses, especially if you want to do one of the more popular courses.

B: So you are saying it's hard to find a place at a university with a Foundation Course?

C: No, there is still a lot of choice, just not as much as with 'A' levels.

B: What's the course like, anyway?

C: Hard work! But I've enjoyed it. The one I'm doing combines Business Studies and English, so I study different business modules for 15 hours a week, and then we study Academic English – that's six hours.

B: And what are the English classes like?

C: They're good – I find them really helpful. They're not like the general English classes I was doing before, though. We do a lot of work on reading academic-type texts and writing in the sort of style that you need to use at university. It's quite hard. Even when I feel that the language I'm using is mainly accurate, the thing that's really different to my language is how essays are structured in English. We're doing quite a bit of IELTS practice, too, at the moment, because most of us are planning to take it next month.

B: So you have to take the IELTS exam?

C: Most universities want you to, yes.

B: What's the other part of the course like?

C: The business modules? They're really interesting. We look at economic theory and marketing strategies, global markets, all kinds of things. I had a bit of an advantage, because I studied Business in high school in France and so I know some of the information already, but it's in a bit more depth than I did before and studying it in English makes a big difference. It can be difficult to understand everything that your lecturer says, sometimes. We have a lot of written work to give in too – assignments, mainly.

B: It sounds very hard.

C: And I've got to give a 20 minute presentation next week using Powerpoint …

B: Really?

C: But despite all of that I'm really enjoying it!

B: So have you applied for any universities, yet?

C: Yes, but it's difficult, because the university I really want to go to hasn't given me an offer yet.

B: Which one is that?

C: Ainsley University. I've had a conditional offer from Millford, and they only want IELTS band 5.5, which I'm sure I can get. I've heard that Ainsley usually ask for 6.5, and that's a bit more difficult. Then there's Parmouth, but I haven't heard from them yet, either.

B: Which one is the better university?

C: Overall, Ainsley is, but people say that Millford has a great Business School.

B: What's Millford like as a place to live?

C: Well, it's in Westhampton, actually. I've heard the city is pretty good, but Parmouth is better – it's close to the sea.

Recording 18

Diagram 1

So light rays from the object, which is a small leaf in this illustration, come through the lens to the eye, but because they are diffracted, or bent by the lens, the eye sees a virtual image which is closer and smaller than the real object.

Diagram 2

Pendulum clocks have always been popular. Their technology is quite straightforward, as we can see if we look at this diagram. You can see the hour and minute hands on the front of the clock, we call this the *clock face*, and then if we look behind the face, we see the main gear train, and behind that, the *pendulum*. That's P-E-N-D-U-L-U-M. This is the part of the clock that we hear ticking. This is driven by a weight which is situated in front of the pendulum and by slowly pulling downwards on a string, the weight pulls the gear train around.

Diagram 3

The campus is quite a large one, and most people take a few days to find their way around. The Students' Union is the large, single storey building in the middle of the campus, and the cafeteria is right behind it. You can get to the cafeteria through the Students' Union, or through a separate entrance at the back. If you walk out of the main entrance to the Union, there is a large lawn area that is very popular in the summer, and then, to your left is the library, and over to your right is the Porter Building.

Recording 19

Good morning, everyone. Well, moving on from our discussion last week about oil-fired power stations, I want to move on today to a form of power that many would argue is far superior. It provides 25% of all electricity worldwide and is the only power generator in common use that uses renewable energy – I am, of course, talking about hydroelectric or hydropower plants – energy from water. Hydropower plants are actually based on a rather simple concept – water flowing through a dam turns a turbine, which turns a generator. The idea is nothing more than a water wheel and the principle has been in use for thousands of years.

Some hydropower plants are built using waterfalls, but the majority of them rely on a dam that holds back the water in a river, and creates a large artificial lake, called a reservoir. That's R-E-S-E-R-V-O-I-R. If you look at this diagram, you will see that the main powerhouse is built in front of the dam and that the transformer is inside, seated on the generator. The turbine is situated underground. Sorry, what was that? Turbine, T-U-R-B-I-N-E. Right, as you can see, under the dam there is a control gate, and this can be opened to let the water in. It travels by gravity, through a tunnel, called the *penstock*, to the turbine, and then out of the outflow to the river below the dam. This movement of water turns the turbine, which generates electricity. The amount of power generated can be controlled by the amount of water taken in by the control gate, so that, for example, at night, when less electricity is consumed, the supply can also be reduced. The power is converted by the transformer into very high voltage current, which is then taken to where it's needed by the power lines, shown leading away from the power station.

Recording 20

Let's look at this final process in a little more detail. As we've said, the power leaves the generator and enters what is known as a *transmission substation* at the power plant. This substation uses large transformers to convert the electricity up to extremely high voltages. This may be over a hundred thousand volts. The reason for this is to reduce losses of power when it's transported over very long distances. On average, electricity travels about 500 km from where it's produced to where it's used. That's a long way! The next stage in the process is a local power substation. This has several functions – it 'steps down' the electric voltage, that is, it reduces it to something that can be used domestically, it also distributes the power, and finally, has circuit breakers so that the power can be switched off if necessary. The power coming out of the substation and along wires to houses is still at 7,200 volts, and so, close to each house, is a transformer drum or box, which lowers the voltage to 240 volts – normal domestic electric service. Finally, each house has a fuse box, or a circuit breaker, which are safety devices to ensure that accidents with electricity are minimized in the home.

Recording 21

Let's get back to our hydroelectric plant. One of the main advantages, of course, of generating power in this way, is that it is a very clean and green method. It takes advantage of a naturally occurring process and so there is little pollution caused, and it's sustainable – it will keep going long after coal and oil have run out. However, there are some difficulties. It depends a lot on the geography of the country – obviously a large river is needed with a reliable flow of water and it's often difficult to find a place which is suitable for a dam. Creating a large, artificial lake involves flooding a river valley, and this is not often popular with the people whose homes will be left underwater! Usually people are compensated and resettled – given homes in a new location – but this can cause other social problems.

Recording 22

Good afternoon. Today we start the first in a series of five lectures on the petroleum industry. Today we'll be looking at how oil is formed, and how it's found by oil companies. Over the next few weeks we'll be examining the process of extraction, and of processing, in more depth.

Right, as you know, in the developed world in particular, oil is a vital commodity. In a single month, the demand for crude oil in the USA can be over 400 million barrels. So where does it come from? And how did it get there? Between 10 million and 600 million years ago oil was formed from the remains of tiny plants and animals, mostly invisible to the human eye, called *plankton*. When they died, the plankton sank to the bottom of the sea, into the sand and mud. Because of all of the sand and mud, usually called *sediment*, there was little or no oxygen and so the plankton was broken down to form organic layers. We call this mixture of organic matter and rock, *source rock*. Over millions of years, more and more sediment was deposited, and the weight of these layers put enormous pressure and heat on the source rock. Because of this, the organic matter, which, you will remember was originally from our plankton, was distilled into crude oil, and could flow out of the rock. Some rock, such as sandstone, is very porous, which means that liquid can be absorbed into it, a bit like a sponge. The crude oil collects in rock like sandstone, or perhaps limestone, and it is called *reservoir rock*.

So what we have now is crude oil, inside sandstone, or maybe limestone, under the ground. Now, if you look at the diagram on your handouts, you'll see that this reservoir rock can be trapped in the Earth by various methods. In all three cases, the natural gas and oil is trapped below a layer of hard rock that it can't flow through. This is known as *cap rock*. The first illustration shows *folding*; strong horizontal movements push the rock together into a fold and trap the oil and the natural gas, which sits on top of it. The second drawing shows *faulting*, that's F-A-U-L-T-I-N-G. Here the layers of rock crack, and then, when one side shifts upwards or downwards, the oil is trapped against the fault line. Thirdly, we have *pinching out*. In this case the cap rock comes up from below, and is actually squeezed upwards into the reservoir rock, leaving two pockets of oil.

Finding oil is an expensive business, and although modern technology such as satellite imaging, has made it much easier, the success rate for finding oil fields is still remarkably low. For every ten potential sites found, only one will yield a new oil field. When one has been found, however, there are certain procedures that need to be followed. The first thing is to settle all the legal issues over who owns the land. As drilling is usually in desert areas or the sea, this is not always as straightforward as you might think! After this has been done, the crew start to prepare to drill. Let's look at a land example to give us the idea. Firstly, the land has to be cleared and levelled and access roads may have to be built, depending on what is available. Water is needed for the drilling process, so there must be a source of it locally. If there isn't one, then a well has to be dug. After this, the crew dig a *reserve pit* – basically a big hole lined with plastic to protect the environment. The reserve pit is used to get rid of rock cuttings and drilling mud during the process. Finally, several holes are dug for the rig, and then a large, rectangular pit, called a *cellar* is dug where the actual drilling hole will be. This gives the workers room to move about when they start to dig the main hole. They start doing this with a smaller drill, and then when they have the hole started, the main rig is brought in.

Speaking module

Recording 23

[E = Examiner, S = Student]

E: Why are you taking IELTS?
S: Generally, er, because the universities need it, and, er, need to achieve, er, a high score of English level.
E: How long have you been studying English?
S: Five years. I studied at high school in China.
E: How would you describe your home country or your home town?
S: My home town is, er, charcoal, charcoal town. The product major is charcoal. And um, it's not really nice town, it's industrial town.
E: What are the best things about life in your country?
S: Um, Chinese food … dumplings, something like that.
E: What do you usually do at the weekend?
S: I usually do, play ping pong and swimming in China, and go to fitness clubs.
E: What do you hope to do in the future?
S: I want to be a managing director.

Recording 24

OK, the important day in my life that I'm going to talk about happened about four years ago. This was the day my football team got promoted. The team, er, had played well all that season and had reached the finals and my brother and I were, er, were both keen supporters and we both followed the team, er, for about fifteen years. It was a very exciting day for, for the team because they'd never been promoted out of the division into a higher division in their history.

My brother and I got into the football ground about lunchtime and waited for the game to start as the crowd built up – there were about 10,000 people there that day. The game swung from side to side, with , first of all, our team scoring and then the other team scoring twice, which was why it was fantastic when our team scored two goals in the last five minutes to win the day and gain promotion to the higher division. The noise at the final whistle was amazing and we were all incredibly excited. I don't think I've ever been to a game where there was such a great atmosphere, before or since. We really celebrated that night, but the next morning, I could hardly speak from all of the shouting I'd been doing!

Recording 25

Student 1

I met my friend in China six years ago. My parents and his parents are, um, workmates and he and me are, were, classmates in high school. And, um, he's in England for three years, and so am I. Er, we study together and live together as well. He studies harder than me and he's, er, very generous and he's, er, quite intelligent as well. So he plays a very important place in my life.

Student 2

OK. I have a friend called Jolie. She's Chinese and we met in the first class, the first English class. We were paired up to do an assignment and that's how we became friends. Umm… I've known her for about five months and it's been fun. We do…we help each other assignments and we go for movies and cook together, have dinners and stuff and just have fun talking, laughing and singing. Um… I think she's played a very important part in my life because she…she…I admire her motivation and dedication and I think she's a very intelligent person and very strong-willed and …something… a lot of her character I wish I had in my life so that's why I think she's played an important role in my life.

Recording 26

1 A: Do you enjoy playing sports?
   B: Yes, definitely. I particularly enjoy outdoor ones.
2 A: Would you like to go there again?
   B: Possibly. It would depend on who I went with!
3 A: Do you think it will be easy to get a job in IT?
   B: I expect so. It's a growing industry.
4 A: Have you ever been to any other countries in Europe?
   B: Yes, a few. France, Spain and the Czech Republic.
5 A: Would you consider doing the same sort of job again?
   B: I don't think so. It wasn't really for me.
6 A: Would you recommend the holiday to other people?
   B: No, not really. It wasn't very good value for money.

Recording 27

[E = Examiner, S = Student]

1 E: Do you think smoking will be banned in all public places?
  S: It's hard to believe that, because, people in China, not like in England, when they drinking and eating, they probably like to give you a cigarette to smoke, and I would like to stop smoking in public buildings and public libraries, because it hurts the people.

2 E: Do you prefer to go out or stay at home in the evenings?
  S: I prefer to stay in, because after class I feel very tired.

3 E: Do you think that email has made our lives easier?
  S: Mm, yes, I think so, because email makes distance, um, shortly, makes distances reduced and, um, you can connect your friends where ever he or she is.

4 E: Which is better: living in the countryside or in the city?
  S: I much prefer to live in the countryside. It's quite quiet there, and the fresh air is very, very good.

5 E: Are qualifications important?
  S: For my opinion it's not really important, well, it is important in China, but personal ability is much more important, because in people's eyes, your goals can be anywhere.

6 E: How likely is it that computers will be able to do your job in future?
  S: Um, all jobs to do with calculation and, um, numbers, but I don't think computers can help us to think about things.

7 E: Would you rather watch sport or play it?
  S: I do like to play it. I like to play basketball and swimming. Yes, I do like to watch it as well, but not really, you know, strong as to play it.

8 E: What do you think the consequences of global warming will be?
  S: Mm, actually I don't know much about global warming, but I think it's a really pollution to take very seriously.

Practice test

Section 1

[JT = John Taylor, EA = Estate Agent]

EA: Good morning, William's Estate Agents. Julie speaking. How can I help you?

JT: Oh, hello, um, good morning. I'm new to the area, and I'm looking for a flat or a small house to rent. Do you deal with rental properties?

EA: Oh yes, we have quite a number of properties for rent. What area are you looking for?

JT: Well, I've only recently moved here, so I don't have any definite area in mind, but I'm studying at the university, so I'd like to be within a reasonable distance of that.

EA: Is that Aston University, or Birmingham?

JT: Birmingham.

EA: Oh, OK, and what sort of thing were you looking for?

JT: As I said, a flat or a small house – there's only me, so I don't need a lot of space.

EA: One bedroom, then?

JT: Probably two – I'm doing a Masters degree, and I find it easier to work at home, so I'd like to have an extra room for a study.

EA: Do you want a garden or a garage?

JT: No, not really. A garden would be nice, but it's not essential … oh, and I don't have a car.

EA: And what sort of price were you looking to pay?

JT: I don't really know what price properties go for around here, but I guess my limit would be around £500 a month.

EA: Well, I've got a couple of things here that might suit you. There's a ground floor flat that's within walking distance of the university, in Edgbaston and a flat in Moseley which is on the, er, third floor.

JT: Sorry, did you say Moseley? How do you spell that?

EA: M-O-S-E-L-E-Y.

JT: Thanks. Is that far from the uni?

EA: No, not very far, and there's a direct bus there, which runs pretty frequently, I think. Moseley's a nice place to live, too.

JT: Are they furnished?

EA: The one in Moseley is fully furnished, but the other one isn't.

JT: How much are they?

EA: The one near the uni is £480 per calendar month.

JT: OK. And how much is the flat in Moseley?

EA: That's £520 a month.

JT: That's a bit more than I want to pay.

EA: I know, but it's a really nice flat. I think you should have a look at it.

JT: Does the rent include any bills?

EA: All of our properties have water rates included, but gas, electric and phone – they're your responsibility I'm afraid.

JT: OK. When can I view these places?

EA: When is convenient for you?

JT: I'm pretty flexible and I'd really like to find somewhere quite soon.

EA: How about this afternoon?

JT: Great.

EA: Why don't we meet at the Moseley flat, and have a look at that, and then we can go on to the other one afterwards.

JT: Good. So what's the address?

EA: Have you got a pen? Good. It's 375 Greenfield Road, that's G-R-E-E-N-F-I-E-L-D all one word, Road and it's just off the High Street. Meet me outside the front door and I'll take you up to the third floor to see the flat.

JT: Fine.

EA: Have you got a mobile phone number, too in case anything goes wrong?

JT: Of course. It's 0791 357629.

EA: Sorry, did you say 619?

JT: No, 357629. Great. Well, I'll see you there at, um, would three o'clock be OK?

EA: Oh, I'm sorry, I've actually got an appointment with another client at three. Could we make it 4.15?

JT: Yes, that's fine.

EA: Good. 4.15, it is then, Mr …

JT: Taylor – John Taylor.

EA: I'll see you then.

Section 2

Good afternoon. It's good to see so many of you here. I hope that you're all settling down well here in Sydney. I'm here this afternoon to talk about one of Sydney's most famous assets – the beach! There are many beautiful beaches in the city, and you can have a lot of fun at them, but it's wise to be aware of a few things when you're there.

You've probably heard about shark attacks, but in fact, they're pretty rare. Usually it's surfers, who are quite far out in the water. It's true that there are about two or three attacks a year, but if you think about the number of people who swim on the coast, the chance of getting bitten is very small. Another marine hazard are box jellyfish which can give you a very nasty sting, but they're only really a problem further up the coast where the water is warmer, say from about Brisbane onwards.

Some of you, I know, are from climates much warmer than here, but for those of you who aren't, the sun is very strong here, especially in the summer months, and you should be really careful to slip-slap-slop, as we say here: slip on a shirt, slap on a hat and slop on some sun cream.

Finally, something that's much less well-known – rip currents in the ocean. You are far more likely to die in a rip current than any other way on the beach. What's a rip current, then? Well, if you're swimming in the sea and you suddenly notice that you are being pulled out to sea very fast, then you're probably in a rip current. It can be a terrifying experience – one minute you are swimming around quite happily, and the next, you're in the middle of a very strong current that is taking you away from the shore.

So what do you do? Well, most people panic and start trying to swim back towards the shore. This is the worst thing you can possibly do. You'll use up a lot of energy – and being in a panic will make the situation even worse – you'll become totally exhausted, and then it's far easier to drown. So that's the first message. Don't try to swim against it.

Secondly, don't panic. As long as you are relaxed, you'll conserve your energy. Usually, rips are quite narrow and run straight out, at right angles to the beach. So, instead of swimming towards the shore, swim parallel to it, across the current. This should take you out of the rip, and then you'll be able to come in to the shore. Sometimes, the current might be very strong, and you won't even be able to swim across it. However, the further you get away from the beach, the less power the current will have. When you feel the pull getting weaker, you can start swimming again, across the current, and you'll find that the waves will take you back to shore.

The best way to fight rip currents though is to follow a few basic rules. Never go swimming in the ocean alone, and if you're not a very strong swimmer, stick to shallow waters. Better still, only swim in places where there is a lifeguard. Enjoy the beach, and be safe.

Section 3

[A = Andrew, B = Balvir]

B: Hi Andrew. How's your new course going?

A: Biology? It's great – much better than Chemistry. I'm really glad I swapped.

B: What are you up to?

A: I'm trying to get prepared for the Biology presentations tomorrow.

B: Have you finished? I've got to do one for Business Studies, next week.

A: Well, sort of. I'm still struggling with which order to put things, but I know what I've got to say.

B: What's it about?

A: It took me ages to come up with a topic, but finally, I decided to look at an example of selective use of pesticides on crops.

B: Wow, that sounds impressive! What does it mean, exactly?

A: Well, you know that farmers use all sorts of chemicals on their crops, and a lot of them are for killing insects. A lot of the insects are a problem, they reduce yields and cause blemishes on the crops …

B: Like spots on apples, you mean?

A: Yes, exactly like that – or cotton is a good example. If it has any insects in it, or if they have damaged it, it's worth a fraction of what the farmer can get if it's perfect. It makes a huge difference to his profit margin. Of course, the down side to chemicals is that they're expensive, so that cuts into the farmer's profit too, but not as much.

B: So, the farmer wants to kill all the insects?

A: Yes, and no. In most cases, that's what happens. The farmer sprays an insecticide, a chemical that kills everything.

B: So what's the problem?

A: The problem is that some of the insects that are in the field are beneficial to the farmer – maybe they eat the harmful bugs, or maybe they help to pollinate the crop, or something like that.

B: Mm.

A: And so, the problem for the farmer is that they want to be able to kill insects selectively.

B: Is that possible?

A: It is, but it's difficult. I found this one example that I really liked, and that's what I want to talk about in my presentation. It's so clever.

B: OK, so tell me about it. You can practise for tomorrow.

A: Well, it's an example from a farmer with fruit trees. Think about the kind of insects that you don't want on fruit – all of the ones that crawl about – caterpillars, snails, that kind of thing.

B: Beetles?

A: No, usually they're OK. The ones that you do want all have wings – bees, wasps, butterflies, most beetles too.

B: Yeah, so how can you kill one lot and not the other?

A: This is where it's so clever. The farmer paints a ring of insecticide around the trunk of the tree.

B: But won't that kill everything?

A: Only any insects that touch it. Now the farmer sprays the tree with a natural pyrethrum.

B: A what?

A: Pyrethrum – it's a kind of insecticide made from flowers. It doesn't really kill insects, it just stuns them so that they fall out of the tree.

B: All of them?

A: Yes, all of them. Now the insects with wings – the good, useful insects – they will just fly back up to the tree afterwards, but the crawling insects will try to get up the tree trunk, and will come into contact with the other insecticide, and die.

B: Wow, that's clever. I think that that should work well for your presentation tomorrow.

A: I hope so. I'm going to talk a bit about insects becoming immune to insecticides too.

B: Well, good luck. I'm sure it'll be a really interesting talk.

Section 4

Last week we looked at the stock market and how it functions, and so, today, I want to go on to look at business ownership and corporations – what they are, and some reasons why they are formed.

I'd like to start by talking about two different types of business ownership. If you start a restaurant by taking your own money to buy the building and the equipment, then what you've done is formed a sole proprietorship. You own the entire restaurant yourself. You get to make all of the decisions and you keep all of the profit. If three people pool their money together and start a restaurant as a team, what they have done is formed a partnership. The three people own the restaurant themselves, sharing the profit and decision-making.

A rather different way of setting up a business is to become a corporation. Any business that wants to sell shares of stock to a number of different people does so by turning itself into a corporation. This is in all legal ways like a person, and it can act as an individual acts. It's registered with the government, it can own property, it can go to court to sue people, it can be sued and it can make contracts. By definition, a corporation has stock that can be bought and sold, and all of the owners of the corporation hold shares of stock to represent their ownership. So, for example, if I buy ten per cent of the shares of a certain corporation, then I have a one tenth ownership of the company.

There is a whole body of law that controls corporations – these laws are in place to protect the shareholders and the public. These laws control a number of things about how a corporation operates and is organized. For example, every corporation has a board of directors. It's unlikely, but even if all of the shares of a corporation are owned by one person, then that one person can decide that there will only be one person on the board of directors, but there is still a board. The shareholders in the company meet every year to vote on the people for the board. The board of directors makes the decisions for the company. It hires the officers of the company, for example, the president, makes the company's decisions and sets the company's policies. The board of directors can be thought of as the brain of the company – they don't do any of the work of the company, but they make the important decisions.

Let's look at this flow chart of how a corporation works. Firstly, of course, a business idea has to be generated. It's often something that needs a lot of capital, and one of the big reasons why corporations exist is to create a structure for collecting lots of money for investment in a business. Let's say that you would like to start your own airline. Most people cannot do this, because an aeroplane costs millions of dollars. An airline needs a whole fleet of planes and other equipment, plus it has to hire a lot of employees. A person who wants to start an airline will therefore form a corporation and sell shares of stock in order to collect the money needed to get started. The company might sell one million shares of stock at $20 a share to raise $20 million very quickly. The company then invests the $20 million in equipment and employees. The investors (the shareholders who bought the $20 million in stock) hope that with the equipment and employees, the company will make a profit and pay a dividend.

Another reason that corporations exist is to limit the liability of the owners to some extent. If the corporation gets sued, it is the corporation that pays the settlement. The corporation may go out of business, but that is the worst that can happen. If you are a sole proprietor who owns a restaurant and the restaurant gets sued, you are the one who is being sued. You and the restaurant are the same thing. If you lose the suit then you, personally, can lose everything you own in the process, and this is obviously not desirable.

CD Track Listing

Track 1	Recording 1		Track 17	Recording 17
Track 2	Recording 2		Track 18	Recording 18
Track 3	Recording 3		Track 19	Recording 19
Track 4	Recording 4		Track 20	Recording 20
Track 5	Recording 5		Track 21	Recording 21
Track 6	Recording 6		Track 22	Recording 22
Track 7	Recording 7		Track 23	Recording 23
Track 8	Recording 8		Track 24	Recording 24
Track 9	Recording 9		Track 25	Recording 25
Track 10	Recording 10		Track 26	Recording 26
Track 11	Recording 11		Track 27	Recording 27
Track 12	Recording 12		Track 28	Practice Test Section 1
Track 13	Recording 13		Track 29	Practice Test Section 2
Track 14	Recording 14		Track 30	Practice Test Section 3
Track 15	Recording 15		Track 31	Practice Test Section 4
Track 16	Recording 16		Track 32	Copyright information